Lessons
from Everest

Dr. Tim Warren

ISBN: 1453676716
ISBN-13: 9781453676714

Table of Contents

Introduction
Man's mind mars mountain...in Maine

*"In every walk with nature, one
receives far more than he seeks."*

— John Muir

Maybe we took the wrong trail and I won't have to go over the Knife Edge,
I pleaded to myself for the thousandth time. My Newfie friend Bob
Healey and I were scrambling up the rocky east face of Mt. Katahdin
in mid-state Maine. The forty-mile-per-hour wind gusts amplified my
near-paralyzing unease. An ever increasing sense of dread constricted
my chest, making each breath labored and shallow. My lungs felt as if
truck transmissions were chained to each lobe. I was terrified.

It was July 1992 and I had a four-year-old chiropractic practice, a
three-year-old marriage, and a one-year-old son. I had been an endurance athlete since the age of twelve and a hiker since I could walk. With
family and business constraints, I could get FWA (full wife approval)
for one three-day backpacking trip per year. This was that trip ... and
I was hatin' it.

Bob had driven south from Canada, and I north from Rhode Island
to climb Katahdin's Knife Edge together. The Knife Edge is one of the
most famous hikes in the Northeast. Although only a smidge over a
mile long, as the name implies, it is frightfully exposed. The elevated
catwalk connects two lesser summits, Pamola and Chimney, of Maine's
highest point at 5,267 feet. The trail has huge drop-offs on either side.
We were told by the twenty-something park ranger we met on the
climb that, if a climber falls or is struck by lightning, his or her chance
of survival was miniscule.

I had come up a day before Bob, and had in fact, summitted the
mountain alone the previous day by the non-scary Hunt Trail. Hunt
was part of the Appalachian Trail System and traditionally 'Thru' hikers, as they are called, end their odyssey on Baxter Peak (true summit
of Katahdin), the terminus of the two-thousand mile slog from Georgia
to Maine. The Knife Edge trip sounded like a great idea while planning
the excursion in the comfort of my sea-level living room.

I had a secret I failed to disclose to the unsuspecting Bob: I was terrified of heights. I had taken one disastrous rock-climbing class with buddy Dana Millar several years before. Twenty feet above the ground I had become so "gripped" with fear that I was frozen to the rock – couldn't go up and couldn't go down. Gradually, the instructor talked me into moving. I swore to never put myself in that miserable position again. I had mistakenly thought that the passage of years would some-how cure me of the dreaded "grip". Alas, the overwhelming fear that had tethered my muscles and mind into stasis was alive and well.

I hate this. I hate this. Why did I do this to myself again? I bemoaned silently. I almost had myself convinced that we were on the wrong path and I would be saved the embarrassment of admitting my weakness to Bob. After some hours we crested a stony plateau and arrived at Pamola Peak and gazed for the first time at "The Edge". The route looked more trapeze than trail. The broken towers of rock that fell away for hundreds of feet below had a lunar essence, more dead than alive. *Shiiiiiiiiittt,* I cursed under my breath. Of course we had taken the correct path. I had known it deep down the entire day. Fear stared me in the face and there was no escape, even in the comfy recesses of my mind.

We started across, or should I say, Bob started across. I took one step and was brick-walled by immobilizing fear for five minutes before venturing another step. The route was exposed, yes, but had handholds and footholds that made it manageable. I would as likely fall off a side-walk as I would this trail. My mind, however, paid no heed. Billions of neural connections flooded my cerebrum with its version of the truth: *I am a dead man if I move an eyelash.*

I was an immobile mess – it was now ten minutes between steps. I insisted that Bob go on without me. I would haltingly retreat to Pamola Peak with my tail between my legs. In addition to the afore-mentioned car parts, my chest now had an engine block attached to it. I retraced leaden petrified steps to the safety of the plateau and there watched Bob skip his merry way across the high wire trail.

I hunkered down among the rocks, out of the wind, and sullenly broke out a snack. I was not alone. A Boy Scout troop of eleven boys and two leaders had just arrived. They offloaded packs and broke out their chow. They were between twelve and thirteen years old and acted it – throwing food at each other and goofing off. I couldn't have pushed the Knife Edge from my mind with a herd of yaks, yet not once was it mentioned, even in passing, by any of the Scouts or the leaders. Were they oblivious to this deathtrap? After twenty minutes the leaders simply shouted, "Saddle up boys let's go." And with that, they just cruised across the Knife Edge without as much as one complaint.

I sat there, mouth agape, dumbfounded. Why wasn't anybody else at least as afraid as I was, or at the very least mildly tentative? Even the frickin' twelve-year-olds traversed the route as if they were skipping their way to junior high gym class. Why was I such a basket case?

Then I got it, it was my head. My mind was sabotaging my life. And all this time I thought my head was on my side. I vowed that I would learn to make my mind an asset rather than allow it to function as the arch enemy of enjoyment, accomplishment and success. At that moment, I realized the critical importance of balance – mental, physical and chemical – in one's life.

I am far from a Latin scholar, but the phrase "mens sana in corpora sano" suddenly made sense. It meant "sound in mind and body." I had no plans to do more climbing, but it was clear that life would bring plenty more opportunities for mind and body to successfully play on the same team. I was right, especially in the dimensions of work, love, fatherhood, social, physical, financial and spiritual. And, in 1993, I very quietly started climbing again.

Not in my wildest dreams could I fathom that nearly eighteen years to the day I would indeed be climbing again, this time on my second attempt of Mt. Everest. The highest point on earth and the "Holy Grail" for mountaineers everywhere (even the armchair variety). I had learned a valuable lesson on "The Edge" but as it turned out that was just the beginning.

My hope is that you, my reader and fellow climber of life, are inspired by the following words, and as your tanks may dwindle, my story in some small way becomes your virtual Sherpa, leading you on with quiet confidence to your chosen Everest.

"The greatest discovery of any generation, is that a human being can alter his life by altering his attitude."
— William James

Chapter One
Dream Management

"You are led through your lifetime by the inner learning creature, the playful spirited being that is your real self. Don't turn away from possible futures before you're certain you don't have anything to learn from them."
— Richard Bach

Mt. Everest Base Camp, May, 2007, 17,300 feet. Painful indecision. Sleepless days and nights. Violent hacking cough. Lungs and throat raw meat. Fear of what was to come. Fear of the route above Camp Three. Fear of the catwalk between the South Summit and the Hillary step. No energy to face down the fear.

Have I done my best? I should have trained more intelligently. Is my mind in the way? Am I talking my way out of a summit bid or are my fears warranted? Discord on the team. *I am sick. I shouldn't go on, but this is Everest. Maybe I should just come back next year. What about my sponsors? What will they think about failure? Will they support another attempt? Were Tuck and Jangbu politely telling me to stop the attempt? Maybe I am just not cut out for Everest.*

Alone in my tent, most of my teammates, including Al, my climbing partner, were on their own summit attempt. Lonely. I missed my son Kurt. If I were with him then he would have called me a "tool" for thinking that way, and he would have been right.

After all, there is no failure on "The Big E" (unless you die that is). To try to heal my finicky lung tissue, I decided to go lower, to thicker air. I walked "down valley" with a hacking, tissue-ripping cough to Pheriche (14,000 feet) where I met up with teammates Nat, Ryan and the two barrister Brits at the Himalayan Hotel under the smiling, always gracious, proprietorship of Ang Nuru Sherpa.

When the temperature dropped below freezing at five p.m., Nuru's young Sherpa helpers lit the yak dung firebox and the climbers and trekkers filed in, speaking Russian, Czech, French, Romanian, English and Nepali. By then, we were all ravenous for a dinner of mo-mos a thin pasta covering cheese or meat, and vegetable picadas, a deep-fried bite-sized entre that came with a ketchup-like dipping sauce. What a place to relax, with funky reading material donated by decades of international trekkers (donate a book and get fifty percent off the room rate of two hundred rupees or about five bucks American) and the finest milky sweet tea. The Himalaya was just what I needed. I could rest, eat and read all day, then write out a dispatch to send on hand-held computer and satellite phone each night to the thousand or so people in the States following my blog.

After a few days when my buddies left for Base Camp and the summit, I was still not healed. In fact, I kept others up at night in the thin-walled rooms with my relentless, rib-rattling "Khumbu cough", caused by many weeks of forcefully sucking in thin, dry, frigid air nearly devoid of oxygen.

Each night I resorted to swallowing codeine pills which I had broken up into quarters to manage the violent hacking. I loathed taking the drug as it depresses respiration; hardly a happy thought when, even at Base Camp, there is one-half the oxygen available at sea level. At this altitude, the simple act of tying your shoelaces is exertion enough to cause you to pant like a hyperactive foo-foo dog. But I couldn't sleep a wink without the codeine, and I was conscious of people around me getting ticked-off from lost sleep.

I called Tuck and Jangbu, the International Mountain Guides (IMG) management team at Everest Base Camp, and informed them of my intention to go even lower down valley, all the way to Deboche at 12,500 feet. Lower altitude meant more oxygen, which meant more pulmonary healing, which meant a shot at the summit, my ultimate goal.

I learned from Amy, a climbing guide for Alpine Ascents, of the Ama Dablam View Inn, a relatively clean teahouse with good (safe) food and a blue metal roof. Such recommendations were vital in the Khumbu Valley of Nepal, because western hygienic food prep can be hit or miss in the teahouses. One speck of spoiled yak cheese can result in gastro-intestinal disasters that have hamstrung many a summit attempt in the Third World.

Each step of my solitary hike became progressively more exhausting. I felt no energy or elation with the increased oxygen concentrations. I felt trashed physically and psychologically as I made my way for hours down valley into an increasingly green, lush world of flowering rhododendrons. The views were heaven on earth but I hardly noticed because of the mental battle raging in my head over the fear of what was to come. Hiking alone I had time, too much time, to think about what I had undertaken.

I had read about Everest since I was a kid. I had thought about, planned, and devoted much of the previous four years preparing for this expedition. I was on a mission. A selfish mission, some might say. After all, I had spent a terrific amount of money, time and energy on myself. Add to that the undeniable possibility of death, and to some this mission probably seemed absurd.

As I walked down the narrow nine-hundred-year-old path, I realized my sense of mission had become dulled, clouded, by my hacking cough, my exhaustion, but most of all by my overriding sense of fear. For several days since becoming ill at Base Camp, and as I trudged down the dusty path, I felt Everest looming over me like a giant avalanche about to bury me in its depths. I could not, for the life of me, visualize myself standing on the summit of Everest. There I was trying to go to a lower elevation to rest and get healthy so I could go to the highest of elevations, but when, I thought of going up, I just couldn't "see" myself succeeding. I had lost my mountain mojo.

I came into a small village and almost immediately saw the roof and sign. *Can this be it?* It certainly didn't seem very prosperous, but I trusted Amy, who assured me she had stayed there on each of her many Everest expeditions.

As soon as I hesitated a moment in the stone veranda in front of the two story ramshackle teahouse, a young Sherpa woman with baby-in-backpack handed me a cup of steaming milk tea as I off-loaded my yellow Wild Things pack stuffed with my forty-below-zero down sleeping bag, toiletries, snacks and clothes. *OK,* I thought, *this had better be it.*

She showed me to a room on the first floor that had no furniture except a wooden sleeping platform with ornate woolen rug on top for insulation and padding. The walls, made of quarter-inch paneling, displayed gaudy plastic Asian pictures, the Nepali equivalent of Elvis on velvet.

Windows in the upstairs glassed-in dining area revealed quaint, pastoral views of a mist-covered valley, a spitting image of Tolkien's Shire. Farmers with hand tools tilled the brown, dusty fields which fill every tiny patch of earth available. Letting my gaze rise higher, I saw great glacier-laden ramparts clinging to the twenty thousand foot foothills beyond the village. I couldn't make out the namesake mountain, Ama Dablam, clouded as it was with fog and coming rain.

I ordered up some food and it hit me - I was the only guest. I got an immediate pit in my stomach and wondered once again if I was making a huge mistake. The innkeepers were devoutly Buddhist based on all the paraphernalia: incense burners, rattles and ceremonial copper bowls of all shapes and sizes. The ubiquitous old climbing expedition posters and advertising stickers also abounded. The Sherpani told me that her husband, like all the men of age, was off on some mountain expedition leaving the aged father and mother to run the house and help with the young baby. The old couple politely asked questions about where I was from and what I was climbing, even though we could each understand only ten percent of the conversation. They clucked apologetically when I told them that I was ill and hoped to improve enough to attempt Everest. Again, I wondered if I was in the right place and if I could trust the food. I ordered only heavily fried and cooked goodies.

My task from the expedition's first day was to overeat as much as possible since muscle tissue wastes at high altitude even when doing absolutely nothing. At Base Camp, you can lose weight just by sitting around because your heart labors as if you were running nine-minute miles. I took a long luxurious nap, got up, and ate more. I rationed lozenges and hard candy for my raw throat. Before leaving Pheriche, I had stopped at the HRA (Himalayan Rescue Association) for an exam of my fragile throat condition. The volunteer British doc couldn't do much. Yet here at lower altitude, my cough seemed a bit better. I was still on the codeine but needed less of it to get some rest. My plan just might work out.

I couldn't get a radio connection to Base Camp and constantly fretted about the weather window. There are very few days a year, usually in late May, when the weather conditions are benign enough to attempt a summit of Everest. Climbers must be prepared in every way to take advantage of that opportunity. I decided to leave in the morning, having spent two nights with the Sherpa family at lower altitude.

At dinner, the baby crawled about the dining area, getting into trouble by playing with the Buddhist objects and I was struck by the similarities of kids all over the world. I read and wrote in my journal as the baby played at my feet. I would have enjoyed being here a heck of a lot more if I didn't have so much fear and uncertainty on my mind. I slept fitfully that last night. My objective was to head back up, way up, to the top of the world seventeen thousand feet higher. I needed my body and mind to play nice together for the ordeal to come. They weren't.

Jim, a fellow climber from our expedition, was a character who quit his high-tech marketing job to climb Cho Oyu, the world's sixth highest peak, and Everest, in the same year. He had accomplished the former the previous October. On Everest, he also got whacked with the Khumbu cough. He had hiked down valley before me, and one day we crossed paths on the dusty yak path just below Pheriche. He was heading up and, I, down. While we chatted in an increasingly biting wind and snow squall, he told me that to save energy he had hired a porter to carry his pack. *Hmmmm, that's an idea.*

I asked the innkeeper if he could hook me up with a porter all the way back to Base Camp so I could save vital energy. We agreed on fifteen-hundred rupees (about twenty-five bucks) for a porter to Base, including a night in Lobuche. My bill for two nights and five meals was seventeen-hundred rupees and the old inn keeper seemed surprised that I didn't complain. He happily presented me with a suundi, a thin red cord blessed by a lama, or high priest, for good luck that is worn around the neck. For improved karma, you are supposed to leave the cord on until it rots off. It was my second suundi of the trip, the first being a gift from climbing partner Phinjo Sherpa (pronounced Pin-jo) when we first met at Namche Bazaar weeks earlier.

Sherpas are the ethnic group in the Khumbu Valley and Everest area who originally migrated from Tibet three to four hundred years ago. They are highly regarded expedition team members and elite mountaineers. We "mikaroos" (non-Sherpas) would have little chance for success on Everest without their expertise. Sherpas are virtually all devoutly Buddhist and also believe in numerous gods and demons who reside in the mountains, caves and forests. Tibetan Sherpas call Everest "Chomolungma" and Nepalese Sherpas refer to her as "Sagarmatha" and both mean "Goddess Mother of the World."

The many Sherpas I had gotten to know over the years were, without exception a fun friendly bunch who sported brimming wide smiles. The smiles come from the heart, but also showcased the whitest, most perfect teeth imaginable, attained mostly without a smidge of professional dental care.

The villages in Nepal, at least the ones on the way to Base Camp, had no signs that said "Entering Deboche". I realized that I was mistaken the whole time and was in Pangboche (13,000 feet), rather than Deboche (12,500 feet), the whole time. Maybe there were multiple Ama Dablam View Inns with blue roofs. *Whatever ... it's all good.* I later learned that Pangboche was the oldest Sherpa village in Nepal.

I felt a bit smarmy and embarrassed when I met my porter, a Sherpani woman of similar age to the young mom at the inn. I was a healthy looking American man, much bigger than she was, yet I was paying her to carry my pack? She was no doubt happy to make the money. I just hoped not to see many climbers along the way. She was wrapped in the traditional Nepalese dress of thick wool, dyed dark brown and ochre, together with the striped apron on front and back (signifying she was married), and wore Nike running shoes. She shouldered my pack along with her small personal bag as I said my goodbyes to the innkeeper family. As we started to hike, the terrain was only moderately steep but my respiration rate was red-lined.

The weather had been rainy and mild for the previous two days, but now we trudged uphill in fog and wind with the occasional snow squall. I soon started to wretch and hack with the exertion and elevation gain. At times, I had to stop until a bout of head-spinning vertigo passed and, each time, I was dangerously close to vomiting. After all my plans to get healthy, and enduring the embarrassment of having a small woman carry my pack to conserve energy, I realized my lungs were, at best, minimally improved. Hours later we reached Pheriche and I stopped in again at the seasonal, makeshift health clinic, knowing full well that there was nothing the doc could do.

When I coughed and coughed again, my young porter looked at me with concern but we conversed little since she essentially spoke no English. On the plains above Pheriche, there was good radio reception so I called Tuck (Mark Tucker the head honcho of our International Mountain Guides Everest team). He asked me how I was and I blurted out *In no shape yet to climb Everest.* He suggested if that was true, there was no sense in coming up the 3,300 feet to Base Camp. I agreed and decided on the spot to stay at Ang Nuru's for another day or two and then carry my own pack, coughing or not. I paid the young woman who was thrilled, as I gave her the agreed upon amount for our abbreviated journey together. I'd rather carry my own pack, coughing or not. It was less a macho testosterone-laden decision and more a desire to do it all myself.

Back to the oasis of Himalayan Hotel where I was a veteran of sloth. That night after dinner, I retired to my room with a bit of a stomach-ache. I overheard the trekkers next-door, a young British couple having a conversation through the thin walls and I heard the woman vomiting very daintily and quietly. *What an amateur*, I thought as I nodded off to sleep. I awakened at two or three in the morning with severe stomach pain and the tell-tale salivary response of impending hurl. I barely made it out of bed and down the hall to the communal hole in the floor before I lost my stomach contents while roaring like a bull yak in heat.

Payback is a bitch, I thought, for my earlier haughty thoughts of superiority. I cleaned up what I could see in the dull light of my head-lamp but had no illusions that I got it all before I stumbled back to bed. The next day I felt so sick I didn't get out of bed for breakfast, lunch or dinner. Ang Nuru sent a young boy to check on me. It was touching that he noticed my absence but I couldn't move.

I felt so depressed. *This could be the death knell to my summit attempt. Good. No more avalanche of Everest leaning over my head, ready to bury me. No. Can't think that! Never think that! You are here to summit. Get better! You've come too far to think of anything but summiting.*

The war in my head wouldn't go away. Huddled in my sleeping bag, I heard the two voices debating louder and louder. I twisted and turned, then lay still, too weak to fight the battle any more. I heard voices, conversations and laughter, smelled cooking and watched the afternoon shadows cross the wall. The day went on without me. I felt myself slipping away from Everest without climbing above Camp Three.

I only reached 24,000 feet? Why did I come here? What the hell was I thinking? The wasted months of training and fund-raising. Crap. The wasted money. Double crap. The possibly irreversible damage to my practice and the stress on my son. I don't want to think about it anymore, about anything.

How ironic: not ill at the seemingly risky Ama Dablam View Inn but here at the Himalayan Hotel where everybody trusts the chow. For all I knew, even though I meticulously used Purel all the time, I could simply have picked up a speck on a door handle and voila! Done for and done in. I couldn't eat much at all for forty-eight hours until I woke up on the third day hungry. *Good sign, me thinks.* I ate well all day and planned for a departure the next. Bright and early I enjoyed fried eggs, coffee and chapattis and headed out by six a.m. It proved slow and fatiguing work, carrying my own pack. Maybe I should have kept the Sherpani, pride or no pride. First the long trudge to Dugla, then Lobuche, then Gorak Shep, then finally Base Camp where Phinjo waited with a thermos of warm lemon drink. I struggled into Everest Base Camp in the slow lane.

My supposed rest and recuperation in luxurious, thick air had not exactly worked out. Maybe my lungs were a little better but the gastro-intestinal issue had left me without "pop" in the muscles. I hung out for a day and conferenced with Mark Tucker, making my case for more rest and later summit attempt. Mark countered "no can do" as he had to have the Sherpas tear down the upper camps and couldn't support a summit attempt by just one dude and Phinjo.

I went to bed that night feeling the war erupt again: bummed on one hand as I watched my dream evaporate in the rarified air, relieved on some level that Tuck had let me off the hook. The next morning I was happily surprised that I spent the previous night actually sleeping and not hacking and gagging at all, and without codeine. At breakfast I ran into two team members from Singapore leaving for their run up to the summit. I told them my story. "Don't accept Tuck's decision about the camp break down, they tell me, you paid big money to try to summit. Tell him you're good to go. Get going tomorrow."

So I saw Tuck, who was only an advisor to our team, part of the International Mountain Guides organization that ran Base Camp and provided advisors for teams like ours that were self-guided. In other words he had no direct say in what we did. I found Tuck and told him, *Hey, I'm ready to go up.* Funny, as I said the words I could feel the fear melt away. But he surprised me. No, he heard me coughing during the night. Which was just bull to keep me from going up, his way of saying I was not ready.

Screw it, I said to myself, *I'm going anyway. If I get packed up and get my Camps Three and Four food bags ready today, Phinjo and I can make the weather window and I can still get my turn at bat leaving the next morning May 18, 2007 with a summit goal of May 23.*

I talked to Pemba to link up at breakfast and now it was up to me to make things happen. I got my kit ready by preparing my pack and the food bags. The bulk of my warm summit clothes and equipment was still at Camp Two from my last acclimatization climb. Now it's: eat up, drink up, and rest up to get ready to go way up. After ten days of illness and waffling confidence I once again became goal-oriented and began moving in a positive direction. Body and mind were once again playing nice together. I was running on all twelve cylinders.

Three a.m. comes early but not when you have been awake for an hour just chomping at the bit to get going. My nervousness kept me from a huge breakfast, so I just ate what I could keep down. I put harness and head lamp on, and headed to the Puja altar where Phinjo was already lighting up a juniper bough, chanting Buddhist prayers and throwing rice. I added my rice and silent prayers to the ritual and we wordlessly clomped off through camp to the direction of our dreams.

> *"Everything on the earth has a purpose, every disease an herb to cure it, and every person a mission. This is the Indian theory of existence."*
> — **Mourning Dove**

I'm going to introduce three dispatches here, three of the many I sent out to people following my progress on Everest. Sometimes it's easier to write about experiences such as those on Everest at a computer well after they've happened. You have time for reflection, time for feelings to change, even if just a little. But when you write about an experience minutes or hours after it happens, you tend to tell the raw truth. Your blood is still racing; exhaustion and pain invade your thinking, and what comes out is as close as you can get to how you feel at that time. What follows are three actual dispatches that I wrote, some of the most difficult I had to send.

---

18 May, 2007 14:10 18,000 feet Safe but no summit. Felled by a throat infection related to the weeks of violent coughing. It started three days ago and seemed to improve but this morning in sub-freezing air at five a.m. as Phinjo and I climbed the Khumbu ice fall, we both knew it was over. The dry, freezing air combined with heavy panting constricted my trachea, throat and lungs like a vise. I sat down between crevasses, radioed Tuck at Base and ... cried. Poor Phinjo cried too. I knew going in that, in addition to the physical challenge of climbing Everest, the other conflicts and challenges would be inclement weather (It's perfect now for the boys up there), and staying healthy. Ironically, at home I am rarely ill. If I pushed a little further I would have put others at risk who may have had to assist me and I wasn't about to do that (especially in light of the fact that two additional climbers died several days ago). I will say that I have learned great lessons on this Everest journey, in addition to being very proud of what I did accomplish by stepping up to the plate. I went in search of a great "perhaps". Thanks for listening, Dr. Tim. Out

---

19 May 2007 19:36 17,300 feet Following the boys
With my own summit bid over, I was free to follow the boys last night (our team's first). After taking a week to get to Camp Four at 26,000 feet they left at 9:30 p.m. and had beautiful weather as they climbed through the night. I slept an hour on the floor of the communications tent between Ang Jangbu and Mark Tucker who manned the radio and sifted information like expectant parents all night. They have to do that the next three nights as we have that many waves of summit climbers. Benjamin (Mexico) summited at daybreak, followed by Big Al, Canada; "Distinguished" Jim, USA; and Andre, South Africa. They could not have done it without the expert climbing skills of six Sherpas, who also summited. As for me, I stuck my pack on my back

and started the forty mile trek out, leaving early, in order to get lower so my body can heal at lower altitude and luxuriant air. I am by myself with most of my gear being portered out. It's great to see gradually increasing green growing things and all the mommy yaks had calves. They are everywhere. Dr. Tim over and out

---

The truth was, after leaving Base Camp after Al summitted and heading down valley all by my lonesome … I was hatin' it. I knew I did the best I could, made the good, safe decisions I needed to make in the mountains. I was simply cold inside and angry outside. *I never want to see another mountain in my life*, I kept thinking. I didn't even want to see a picture of a mountain for the rest of my life. And I meant it, for awhile. The hours ticked off as I tramped down the glacier's rubble-strewn trail to Lobuche where the yak path turns to dust. Three hours later I stumbled into Pheriche and my third stay at the Himalaya Hotel where that internal war started up again.

Dispatch: Ruminations on fear 24 May, 2007 18:30 4,000 feet
FEAR acronym-"False Evidence Appearing Real." Hey, it's in my nature to analyze the body, mind and spirit of people, places, things, and events that cross my path in this life and fear in relation to my Everest experience has been on my mind. It will be awhile before I have historical perspective but here is the almost present experience re: fear. With other big mountain experiences, (i.e. Denali) I experienced low-level fear that I welcomed as a great safety tool. In fact, I termed that experience "focused fear." I didn't have that experience on Everest in fact, for all my trips through the icefall and over crevasses on ladders and up the Lhotse Face, I experienced no fear. I find this quite interesting in a detached clinical fashion. All that changed in the days before the abbreviated summit bid. The cocktail of illnesses, being down valley from Base, and the loneliness of being away from my climbing buds all probably contributed, but the feeling was simply dread, or to paraphrase a Hunter S. Thompson title: "Fear and Loathing in Pheriche." I have seen it with others and even experienced it myself decades ago when I first started climbing. Sir Edmund Hillary said, *"We do not conquer the mountains; we conquer ourselves."* The long and short of it is, getting up and going at four a.m. on that summit attempt was the hardest thing I can ever remember doing. We threw our rice, passed the Puja Stupa (stone altar) on the right and began the ten minute walk across

the moraine while weaving through tents as our climbing gear jangled and clanked. I wretched once or twice from phlegm build-up before we arrived at the icefall proper and fixed bayonets (put our crampons on). I couldn't tell if I was fast or slow as there were no westerners to judge my speed, just Sherpas (and they never seem to drink, eat or take a breath the whole time you climb). It turns out, slow was an understatement, wretch and cough were also gross understatements. The rest is history, but I was happy because I felt the fear and did it anyway. As old Rhode Island friend Dana would say "I got on the roof." Simply, fear is False Evidence Appearing Real. Dr. Tim. P.S. I am back in Kathmandu waiting several days for a flight out. (First time looking at my body in a mirror. I haven't been this skinny since the ninth grade) — Dr. Tim over and out.

End of Dispatches.

"If we will be quiet and ready enough, we shall find compensation in nearly every disappointment."
— Henry David Thoreau

Twenty-four hours after leaving Everest Base Camp with my tail between my legs, feeling sorry for myself, napping the afternoon away, it hit me ... Bam! Hit me so hard I got up out of my sleeping bag and walked to the window to watch the yaks graze by the Dudh Khosi River. *I can do this next year. I can come back next year and climb Mt. Everest. I can come back, in 2008, learn the lessons from this year, and summit Mt. Everest. I will learn the lessons, come back in 2008, summit Mt. Everest and safely return! I will. I will. I will.*

I felt the blood surging through me, the stream of blood going into and out of my heart, the individual drops engorging my capillaries and fueling my system. I started thinking about Al. You see, Al was so focused, so obsessive; he'd climb bare-foot and bare-butted to the summit and probably not even feel the cold. Well, that's an exaggeration maybe, but not by much. I have to stop right here and tell you about Al.

Al Hancock works in the Alberta, Canada, oil sands, a blue-collar guy, unlike most of the climbers who had the big bucks to even think of Everest. Al was so well-liked and respected at home, he raised all his expedition money where he worked at Sun Corp. and related subcontractors.

Al was so focused; nothing was going to get in his way. Nothing. Under his hard shell, however, he cared about people, something I learned more about on another climb on another continent. There, in Mendoza, Argentina, we became friends for life. I'm glad we were close together on Everest, because I learned a lot from him.

Al wrote to me once about his focused climbing philosophy: "One needs to be a very mentally disciplined person. You need to be able to cut all ties in your mind with your family, work, money and the luxuries of life while on a climb. You have to be in the moment, and that means cutting the umbilical cord to everything. Disconnect. You need to bow down to the art of suffering where cold becomes your friend and your tiny tent becomes your mansion and the mountain your job. I call this flipping the switch."

The following poem was written by Big Al, no stranger to high self esteem. "When the stars are out, I go to work. When the sun is at its highest, I take a rest. I melt snow from which I drink. I climb to the edge of the abyss. I share creation. Kings can do no more."

Still half-asleep from the nap, I looked out at those yaks, and the voices started the war again. Part of me was a loud roar doin' the hatin', the other, a firm smooth voice patiently and analytically clicking off the reasons why, if I returned next year, I would have a great shot at summiting Mount Everest. Mount freakin' Everest!

More clearly than at any time during the trip I saw myself at the summit and, more importantly, walking back into Base Camp from the top of the world, Safe! And this was the reason: *If Al can do it, I can do it.* He has that focus, that drive that I came to see first-hand. *What the hell's the difference between us — a 200-plus-pound guy, former champion body builder who works in the oil fields and a 160-pound former marathon runner chiropractor?* OK, on the surface there are obvious differences, but why can't his focus be my focus? Did Everest hang over him like an avalanche about to smother him? I doubt it. He probably saw an escalator to the summit with him dancing on the tippity-top. Me? Over those last two weeks I saw nothing but ice, snow, cold and trouble.

Focus: that will be my word. I could finally see myself on the summit standing next to Phinjo as we looked out over the whole blue and white world! *Woo-hoo, the top of the World!*

I had no doubt about it: with my skills, power and motivation and the added jet fuel of experience and confidence, I would learn the lessons and come back to Nepal for the 2008 season, summit Mt. Everest and safely return. This will be my mission and mantra: "Summit and Safe Return."

The second day since leaving Base Camp, I tottered down the trail all by my lonesome to Namche Bazaar, fatigued, hacking phlegm, but thrilled with the plans swirling through my head, the next twelve months of action steps becoming nailed down in my mind. Teammates Andre and Mike from South Africa told me of a teahouse in Namche that had unlimited hot water for showers. I aimed to find this oasis and take the wire brush to my carcass to scrape off the accumulated goop of two months. I checked into what I thought was the place but was once again wrong. A sad trickle of luke-warm water from an archaic faucet greeted me and I realized I would have to wait for a Hotel Tibet shower in Kathmandu to loosen the mixture of dust, sweat and sunscreen that had fused to my epidermis. The plodding continued for eight hours to Lukla the next day, with a shattered body but a soul soaring in the clouds.

One thing gnawed at me, *How will I tell Kurt?* At one of my low moments on the mountain I had e-mailed my handsome then sixteen-year-old and told him I would never climb again. Now I would have to renege only weeks later. How would I explain this? He was thrilled when I had told him of my mountain retirement and, since he kept things close to the vest, what would he really think of his Dad's return to such a harsh life-threatening environment? I ruminated on this quandary for days until arriving back in Rhode Island. I knew I would find the right way, but at that time I had more miles to hike.

Finally, I arrived in Lukla, last stop in the Khumbu Valley before the hair-raising hour flight to crazy Kathmandu and the relative comforts of modern life. It wasn't to be for a few days, however, as the foggy weather closed the airport. I ran into Benjamin, one of our team members from Mexico, who summitted with Al but had hastened down valley to meet his girlfriend. I voraciously pumped him for information on his experience above my highpoint of 24,000 feet. In halting English he explained the reason for his Everest success. "I climb with one mind, not two."

I felt none of my previous crushing fear when he shared the really scary parts of his summit story, because for the first time, I truly saw myself up there, doing what he did. I belonged at the summit. The summit of Everest and a safe return had become, in two days, firmly entrenched as my mission. I was determined to live this dream.

> *"So many of our dreams at first seem impossible, then seem improbable, and then when we summon the will they soon become inevitable."*
> — Christopher Reeve

Why did I not summit in 2007? One reason: the mission was not clear. In 2007, my mission was muddled. Despite all the preparation and expense, I was, simply, not meant to summit. I did not have the necessary tools. When I deteriorated physically, as we all do at high altitude, the mental battle became overwhelming and I skulked back down the mountain. That failure helped me to understand, once and for all, what mission really meant.

"Your work is to discover your world, then with
all your heart, give yourself to it."
— Buddha

I was so hot with my goal to climb Everest in 2008 that I probably had steam coming from under my Red Sox hat. I realized my focus was ill defined, fuzzy and just plain lukewarm the previous year. Of course, my goal was to "climb Everest" but, I never clearly visualized myself at the top. Now I did, and there was not a shred of doubt or indecision in my mind, the vision of Phinjo and me on the top of the world was laser-beam clear. I had it going on. I realized I wouldn't have ever been this hot if not for all the ups and downs and mistakes of 2007. My failure was a prerequisite to success in 2008. It taught me there was no such thing as failure if you learn essential lessons as a result. Failure can be a strange variety of blessing.

"As for the future, your task is not to foresee it,
but to enable it."
— Antoine de Saint-Exupery

Chapter Two
A Warrior Loves His Craft

"Be master of mind rather than mastered by mind."
— Zen Proverb

As a kind of Nepali send-off, our team had an epic, dramatic, terrifying, nearly disastrous exit from Hotel Tibet to Tribuhaven International Airport in Kathmandu. Just as we prepared to go to the airport, the Maoist rebels started one of their near daily confrontations, paralyzing the city and its daily business. We were assured of our safety, as no one wanted to put tourists, the lifeblood of the national economy, at risk of being hurt or killed in the crossfire.

Al, Steve, Jim and I piled into the back of a twenty-person bus with our duffels secured to the roof, and we held our huge backpacks on our laps. Steve and I were in the two back seats. The bus crawled through the now-deserted streets and picked up other tourists. Gradually, the bus got full, then overfull, then people rode on top and hung off the sides. Huge banners on all sides of the bus designated it as "Tourist Only" but these became covered up. Suddenly, we came around a corner to a mob of demonstrators completely blocking the road with rocks, logs and fires. The drivers in the cramped operator area — there must have been four people hanging over the wheel so it was impossible to tell who was actually driving — quickly turned down a side street.

We glanced at each other and breathed a sigh of relief as we dodged the confrontation. The bus picked up speed and we seemed to be well on our way, but when we turned a corner, my heart nearly stopped with horror. The street was completely filled with a mob of angry, screaming demonstrators. A feeling of pure terror engulfed me as I realized there was no escape for the bus or from the bus. It was so overcrowded by now that we were wedged in and intertwined with arms, legs and pack straps. I met Steve's eyes and said, *If things get ugly, we're going to have to break windows and pull each other out.* Steve resolutely agreed.

A hundred or so rebels, dressed in rags, hair greasy, faces filthy and contorted by their angry chants, surrounded and stopped the bus. Many swung bamboo canes over their heads, ready to smash anyone in their way. Several of the mob hurtled into the cab and threw the

15

driver to the ground. The last I saw of him, he was on his knees with his hands together, his voice shrill, pleading for his life. The demonstrators pulled themselves up to the bus windows, taking stock of the passengers. As someone began to let the air out of the tires, one of the passengers jumped into the driver's seat.

Just one thrown rock or some loud noise might well have sparked a volcano of violence, turning us into stains on the road. There would have been no escape if someone firebombed us or sprayed us with machine gun fire. We were a CNN lead story in the making. However, in the ensuing madness, the new driver just gunned the diesel engine; people dove out of the way, and the bus churned itself up the hill. Before we knew it, we were at the airport. One minute, we were praying for our lives, the next we were sitting in front of the terminal. We all sat there for a moment of numbed silence. Then the rush began and we tumbled out of that bus as fast as we could.

Alas, a flight out was not to be. While we encountered the Maoists, our flights had left. After a two-hour wait, we caught another bus back to the now business-as-usual, no harm-no-foul city streets of Kathmandu, and, grateful to be alive, checked back into the Hotel Tibet. We headed straight for the bar.

"Hope for the best, prepare for the worst."
— **His Excellency the Fourteenth Dalai Lama**

June 6, 2007 Warwick, Rhode Island 60 feet elevation. I couldn't wait to get back to my chiropractic office and start adjusting people. Turning the power on, as chiropractors call it. Al and I flew from Kathmandu to Thailand to Hong Kong to Los Angeles to New York City to Warwick, RI, crossed the International Date Line and dealt with a twelve hour time difference over forty eight hours, all the while dozing and watching eight movies. When we landed, each of us wrestled three huge duffel bags and a full backpack through customs.

Back in Rhode Island, my friend Dana Millar picked us up at the airport and we cajoled the poor suffering Big Al back to my house. Big Al planned to stay in Rhode Island a couple of days on the way back to Canada for good reason: he had a case of "Kathmandu colic", otherwise known as "the trots." After the pure guts of summiting Everest on May 19, Al had limped for three days down valley on an injured knee to get to Lukla before flying to Kathmandu. Al made it fine until he caught a nasty gastro-intestinal bug at a hotel buffet and it just leveled him. He slept and ran to the bathroom while setting a new world record for toilet paper use by one bottom. He became so emaciated by the time he got to his girlfriend's home in Toronto that she didn't recognize him. He had morphed into "the Everest climber formerly known as Big Al."

"No defeat is made up entirely of defeat, since the world it opens is a place formerly unsuspected."
— William Carlos Williams

I took a day to do laundry then got back to work and my regular life. I decided to take a slight break from training for two or three weeks to rest and hang with Kurt. At this point in my life, I had been divorced for seven years, did not have a girlfriend and hadn't dated anybody in months. The weather was warm and humid and Rhode Island looked like the lushest of rain forests, especially when I hadn't seen it since the gray days of March.

After only a week, ADHD kicked in and I began serious planning for Everest 2008. My desire to give Everest my best effort was becoming stronger and stronger. The first thing was to organize my training: more emphasis on functional training as well as more scientific cardiovascular work. I had always resisted heart rate monitor assisted training as being too analytical. A heart rate monitor is made up of a chest strap and a watch which the athlete programs to beep if he or she is in the target range of cardio effort. A heart rate monitor is the only way to determine if your training is progressing adequately. It can also give clues if you are over-training.

As a minimally talented high school and college runner, I was a tad wimpy about getting my heart rate up because of the ensuing pain involved. I found I was drawn to the slower, more cerebral, and less painful pace of marathons. As marathons turned to triathlons, then weight training, then all of the above to train for the mountains, I became more comfortable with pain. I should clarify pain as the illusion of pain because pain is relative. I learned to ask myself while grinding up a long hill on my road bike, *Am I in pain?* And the answer invariably would be, *No, it's discomfort*, often strong discomfort, but simply discomfort.

What I had dismissed as too left-brain for me became part of my new commitment. Two days home, I purchased a heart rate monitor and started getting the hang of it. I even embarrassed Kurt when his buddies saw me out chopping wood in shorts, sandals and a monitor.

"Let no one outwork me today."
— Dr. Tim Warren

A Warrior Loves His Craft

In 2007 I thought I'd worked hard in training, but for 2008 I vowed a massive increase. In 2007 former girlfriend Kathy, a retired competitive bodybuilder, had been my quasi-trainer. We did hard workouts but the rests between sets were more related to bodybuilding than an Everest climb. I did a lot of cardio work but evidently not enough. It didn't help that during the last two months before leaving for the Himalayas, I was distracted and pulled in different directions by business issues.

The training felt intense in 2007, but I realized seven thousand miles away that it was not nearly intense enough. For 2008, I decided to train at Northeast Sports Training in Warwick, Rhode Island. The gym was only a mile from my office, but most importantly, Mike, and his bevy of trainers had the goods.

Mike assigned me to Jaime Gamache, a trainer in his early thirties with tattooed quotes of Milton ("abashed, the devil stood and felt how awful goodness is") on bulging biceps, a slightly insane smile, and obligatory sadistic tendencies.

I committed to two workouts a week from July 1, 2007 until I stepped on the plane March 23, 2008. Jaime put me through a "pain-fest" — no rest, constant abuse of multiple body parts, sport-specific functional training. I usually showed up ninety minutes early and got on the step-mill which the club leased for me. I put medicine balls in my backpack and soon became drenched in sweat as I humped uphill without rest. Then I got down to business, flipping the six hundred pound truck tire four to eight reps, then super-setting — jumping in and out of the three foot thick tire without breaking my neck — followed by flipping the two hundred pound truck wheel ten times, plyometric box-jumping while holding the forty-five pound bar in outstretched arms, always doing mass quantities of different exercises to confuse the body. I became known as the "old guy" who worked out like a "madman." I developed a modicum of fame among the high school, college and professional athletes who frequented the house of pain.

Once, doing pushups on differently sized medicine balls, my pectoral muscles gave out and I collapsed chest first onto the hard rubber of an eight pound ball, cracking my ribcage like a lobster shell. For several weeks, Jaime stayed away from upper-body work but managed to find different forms of torture. The whole point was to prepare body and mind for the extreme rigors of climbing asymmetrical ice formations in the unforgiving environment of Everest while utterly exhausted. It's equally important to train my brain for pain, for the mental stress of hours and hours of misery without respite.

I paid Jaime good money for the mountaineering equivalent of water-boarding but it was perfect for where I was going. I focused on forearm strength to hoist myself up a fixed rope; back and biceps to climb vertical ice or rappel off cliffs; hip flexors, glutes, quads and calves to propel myself uphill explosively through the icefall. Under Jaime's watchful eye, I punished my body by working harder and longer than I ever thought possible. My constant mental companions were affirmations such as "pain is weakness leaving the body" and "the purpose of training is to make me hard to kill." I red-lined my body and mind for the next nine months.

Jaime pushed me into severe oxygen debt to increase my body's ability to keep climbing for hour after painful hour in the oxygen-starved atmosphere of the world's biggest bump in the earth.

Afterward, I somehow drove back to the office although I felt seriously dizzy and couldn't grip the steering wheel with my wasted jellyfish arms. I would shower, then collapse on an adjusting table for a catnap before I saw afternoon patients. The ever-driving Jaime claimed, "It's not really a workout unless you have to squirt the shampoo on the shower floor and rub your head in it because you don't have the strength to pick up your arms." I also ran, biked and hiked with gradually increasing poundage of dog food or cement bags inside the backpack.

When the snow started flying, I made regular forays to New Hampshire to ice climb with long time climbing and craziness partner, Rob Scott. Rob and I have had many great adventures together: twice we slogged for weeks up Denali in Alaska, the highest point in North America, where we finally summitted arm in arm in June 2004. Rob, however, does more jonesin' for a fifty foot frozen waterfall. He is the climbing equivalent of Monet to my Jackson Pollock. I prefer the long slogging grind of an expedition, the travel to exotic lands, and the ever-present objective of bagging one of the world's great peaks. Rob, the Impressionist, prefers the more precise, yet more imaginative climbing demanded by picking his way up a strange course of vertical ice.

> *"Cold and exhaustion are mere incidentals*
> *on the road to victory."*
> — Rene Desmaison

The physical was only one of three equally critical parts of preparation and support for the mission. The second is financial, the third, emotional. The physical I have to do myself. I had to rely on others for the other two.

Let me tell you about the financial commitment needed to climb Everest:

- International Mountain Guides — my share of the infrastructure of the climb: $30,500
- Phinjo, my Sherpa climbing mate: $6,000
- Everest climbing permit from the Kingdom of Nepal: $10,000
- Round trip airline ticket from Rhode Island to Nepal: $1,900

Total: Almost $50,000 just to get yourself to the starting line. (Note: climbers who had hired a professional guide or service could spend much more, upwards of $100,000.) My total did not include my training costs or the biggest ticket item: lost income while not working for seventy days.

I had already spent $6,000 on the specialized climbing gear I've gradually accumulated over the years. I made two notable upgrades this year: new down suit and new boots. A suit takes a beating above Camp One — you literally live in it — eating, sleeping and, of course, climbing in the brutal weather conditions above 21,000 feet. I decided on a Feathered Friends one piece for this year. The keys to a good climbing suit are warmth and functionality, and this one, at $1000, fit the bill perfectly. It didn't hurt that it's in the same cool hue of yellow as my Wild Things summit backpack.

The boots ($750.00) are the same as last year's Italian made Millet Everest, triple-layer with high-tech but super-light features that make them look like oversized Frankenstein shoes. Last year's were just too damn big, causing me to repeatedly drive my crampons into one or the other boot leading to potentially life-threatening lurching stumbles, not to mention looking like a drunken Yankee fan. I climbed Mt. Washington in my new correctly-sized boots several times that winter and never spiked myself again, even when dangling from a rope on a vertical frozen waterfall or descending in waist-deep snow.

A couple of smaller but necessary new items: a new headlamp ($80) was imperative. Without light on the greatly exposed Southeast Ridge, ascending or descending is just plain foolhardy. Your carcass could easily freeze into a lump of ice to join the other permanent residents of the upper slopes. I still had my triple-layer oversized OR mitts ($200.00) for the deep cold but needed a snug-fitting pair of ice-climbing gloves for dexterity and warmth. A pair of Black Diamond ice climbing gloves ($95) was best for the serious climbing in the ice-fall to the Lhotse Face and to the summit. If I'm in the sun (a rare occurrence) and it's warm, I'll switch to light ice-climbing gloves to handle ropes and carabiners while keeping the burning sunlight — magnified in the thin air—from scorching my digits. And my "most valuable player" piece of gear — My Patagonia R-1 hoodie, which I knew I'd wear nearly twenty-four-seven — high-tech underwear that wicks any stray moisture but is always warm; it even has a hoodie with offset zipper to prevent any cold metal on the face, a steal at $150. *There is no bad weather…only bad gear,* I often say.

I intended to give my hoodie to Phinjo along with a stuffed duffel of other equipment at the end of the climb, just before the forty mile walk from Base Camp to the plane home. He will need it more than I will, as I have firmly decided that, win or lose, summit or not, this will be my last Everest climb. Phinjo, on the other hand, will climb as long as he can because this was his job and, at thirty-eight, he has a few more years.

Incidentally, the oldest climbing Sherpa on our squad was Dawa, who though still tough as nails was hanging up the crampons at age forty-nine to open a teahouse in his home town of Phortse. It must be difficult for the studly Sherpas who accompany westerners on their climbs in the Himalaya to retire. First of all, they make great ru-pee. Second, they are very proud men. Even though they play Russian roulette with their lives by the sheer numbers game of multiple trips through the icefall, up the Lhotse Face, and to the summit, make no mistake, they want another summit. It's for the personal satisfaction, or juice, as well as being a boon for the pocketbook.

As I write these words, Phinjo has summitted Mt. Everest five times, but he is not even close to Danuru's ten, the most from IMG's group, and will never reach the all-time twenty and counting by the great Apa Sherpa. Ang Jangbu, the CEO of Sherpa activity on our climb, told me that he didn't summit Everest, for various reasons, until his thirteenth try, so it is never a given, even for super-strong Sherpas.

Back to the question of raising money. How do I raise well over $50,000 for the privilege of putting myself in the most challenging environment known to man? If it's anything like last year, I've already learned how. For 2007 I had relished the challenge of approaching businesses and corporations for sponsorship or donations. *How cool is that,* I thought, *your widget showcased on the top of the world by having some knucklehead,* (me), *spend seventy days in god-forsaken conditions, risk-ing death even, just to do it?* My thirty-second elevator speech marketing message to everyone in business who had a pulse was roughly translated to — *I am your knucklehead.* And what do you know?

It worked.

I engaged two big corporate sponsors, Verizon and Pro-Solutions for Chiropractic, and multitudes of smaller companies. I strove to give them back double what they paid for in public relations and visibility. I mentioned them in the many presentations I did, as well as in all interviews for TV, radio and newspapers. I wore Verizon and Pro-Solutions crests on my fleece jacket for six months before leaving, everywhere I went and everything I did.

I was honored that friends, colleagues in chiropractic, and especially patients of mine, were extremely generous. We offered various sponsorship opportunities available from a $15 message on a lightweight sheet that would stay in my pack to the summit, to "adopting" a base camp yak for $250.

Upon returning home in 2007 from my failed attempt and tallying up the damage, we were able to give a $15,000 donation to A Wish Come True Foundation and pay for the majority of the climbing costs incurred.

Based on that success, I naively thought in 2008 I could raise $50,000 for A Wish Come True *and* pay off my $50,000 climbing nut. After all, wouldn't a second try on the world's toughest playground warrant increased interest from advertisers and marketers wishing to place product or service at the world's highest point? Of course, I was thinking, absolutely, *Yes*. But in reality, the most repeated response from previous sponsors, directly or indirectly was, "Why didn't you summit last time?"

I'm still the "knucklehead with a big dream" but somehow less attractive to investors. Pro-Adjuster (the Chiropractic technique that I use) didn't respond in 2008, although Verizon, to its credit, was still on board, albeit for a lesser amount. My friends, colleagues and patients remained wonderfully generous.

As the weeks and months clicked off from summer to fall, 2007, I ramped up the public relations barrage hoping to bring more dollar value to the endeavor. I tried to talk Dan Barbarisi, a *Providence Journal* reporter, into another attempt at a winter climb on Mt. Washington with me. Dan usually writes about politics (a sport in its own right in Rhode Island, home of "lobstas and mobstas"). He had attempted the climb in 2007 with me but he hadn't made the summit due to cold weather and lack of fitness. He wanted no part of another climb and I didn't blame him.

I did radio shows, talk shows, TV interviews, blogs, anything really that could generate publicity for my climb and for A Wish Come

True. Starting weekly in January, I produced a thirty minute show once a week that schools across the country could phone into and use as a lesson plan. I created shows on the Sherpa culture, the climate, fitness and training for the climb, physiology of the body at high altitude, goal setting, and the history of climbing Everest. The show was facilitated by the folks at the Telecom Pioneers, the non-profit wing of Verizon Communications. We ended up with thousands of kids across the country listening and participating each week. It was wonderfully satisfying for me to talk to the kids about Nepal and climbing. But it sparked little in the way of financial support.

Deadlines for payments approached. If I didn't make the payments, I didn't go, as simple as that. Becoming more than frazzled with work in my office, workouts in the gym, and working the phones, I got a little panicky and hired a public relations firm to help me generate interest in the climb. All the company seemed to generate was income for itself. Lots of promises, no dough. Throw out the first puck for the Boston Bruins. Documentary on cable TV. Throw out the first pitch for the Pawtucket Red Sox. I went to Boston for one TV interview, in a limousine, no less. One and done. I went back to doing it myself having spent money I needed for the climb.

By January 15, 2008, faced with the deadline for fifteen grand, I realized something had to give. I had to quit all the hours on the phone. No more butting my head against the wall hustling for dollars. Let me concentrate on training and public relations and forget the fundraising. I also decided to second-mortgage my home and just pay the freight.

> *"Life is expensive, but it does include a*
> *free trip around the sun."*
>
> — Unknown

I always received strong emotional support for my ventures and now preparing for 2008, it was just the same. Co-workers in the office, patients in my practice, close friends and relatives have always wished me well and been very generous. But there were a few close to me who were superstars, the backbone of my emotional support team and I have to tell you about them. My chiropractic practice is always under the watchful, mother hen eyes of Sharon and Joanne, my co-workers for many years. During the months before 2008, they not only gave me their great energy to help work out my crazy schedule, they worked to raise money for A Wish Come True. They didn't blink when, after the years long planning for the 2007 Everest expedition, I promptly laid an egg of a return attempt for the 2008 climbing season. Now that's support.

How, you may ask, can you afford to take two months out of a busy practice and just go "play?" That's another aspect of my life that demanded support. As I did last year, I hired a young chiropractor to take care of the patients while I was gone. Dr. Matt Mendillo was a friendly, competent and ethical chiropractor whom I groomed to have in the practice. He can get a bit long-winded with patients, however, so the girls and I made a plan: as soon as he got a little behind, one of the ladies would sound a chime alerting him. We jokingly had him shaking in his shoes over the sheer horror of this possibility as if it would be a near fatal lapse in his judgment. Giving this young chiropractor some invaluable real-world experience and the ability to get a good paycheck before he opened his own practice was a bonus for him. It was also emotional support for me.

I've saved my two biggest emotional supporters for last. In late July while making a bank deposit, I saw a stunningly beautiful, long-legged woman with dark brunette hair in a fashionable blue summer dress. As I unabashedly stared, I realized I knew her. She was Rose Yehle, and I had heard that she had started a business, "Sewing Creations by Rose." I said hello and congratulations on her business. She stopped and chatted, answering my queries about her new office and business. I had not been aware she was so friendly and sweet. Great smile and eye contact. *Wowser!* Did I mention she was knock-down, drag-out gorgeous?

We went out on a date August 4, 2007, and have been inseparable ever since. She had to put up with a relationship with a guy who loved her very much and was devoted to her totally, but carried the added baggage of unswerving focus on the mission: summit Everest with a safe return. She had to hear my weekly tales of how painful my workouts were and my impending two-and-a-half-month fandango, all of which she had no play in. She endured this process cheerfully and accepted that Everest was the thing I had to do and do it to the best of my ability.

My other emotional supporter was teenage son, Kurt. We took his first nerve-wracked, tentative driving lessons together just before I boarded the plane for Everest in March 2008. While still actively preparing and training, I tried to spend as much time with him as possible.

In late February, Kurt and I took off for a weekend in New Hampshire and stayed at The Nereledge Inn in North Conway, where owners Steve and Laura have taken amazing care of me on multiple climbing and training sojourns. I rented two snowmobiles for the two of us to blast around on. We did our usual North Conway routine of penny candy at Zeb's country store and breakfast of venison sausages at Gunther's. We hung out, laughed and spent precious time together realizing that all too soon the painful separation would begin. Kurt was shocked to be in North Conway in winter and I was not climbing anything.

When I was preparing to leave for Everest in 2007, my little boy was surprisingly fine with me risking my life in a far-off third-world country, saying goodbye with a simple unemotional admonition, classic Kurt: "Dad, don't die." I was unprepared in 2008 when, on our last night together, he completely broke down and cried in my arms saying that he loved me. Having read the misery inflicted on families in *Into Thin Air*, the classic Everest disaster story by Jon Krakauer, Kurt was more aware of the risks to my life than he was in 2007 and I didn't have the larger-than-life Al with me as a teammate. He has never asked me to stop climbing or to skip an expedition; he innately knows that I just have to go. My mission, my purpose, my destiny, my raison d'etre.

"The harder you look, the harder it is to surrender."
— Vince Lombardi

Time marched down toward departure and I crossed myriad tasks off multiple lists. I have often observed that when the mission is the right one, the universe conspires to see it through. Conversely, when striving for a goal is a constant struggle, I now take a long hard look inward to make sure I am on the right path.

My new training regimen had gone well. On one solo foray up Mt. Washington in New Hampshire, I cruised to the summit in less than three hours and descended in one. The windchill was thirty degrees below zero. Washington was a paltry 6288 feet in elevation but had some of the world's worst weather thanks to three converging weather fronts that conspired to rip climbers off the hill and thrash their sorry butts. On average, two people per year die on Mt. Washington's icy wind-scoured flanks.

From my lifetime of training for various endurance sports since the age of twelve, and despite a prodigious amount of weight training, including bench pressing 265 pounds — a hundred pounds more than my body weight, I'll have you know — I have developed a very lean physique, some might say skinny. I therefore needed to gain some weight over the year before returning to Everest. I committed to a

A Warrior Loves His Craft

regime of nutritional habits designed to repair tissue injury resulting from intense training and to add some badly needed bulk to the muscles. Just existing at high altitude causes the body to consume itself, a kind of death-zone cannibalism.

The plan involved five or six meals a day with the definition of a meal being some protein and carbohydrate in a one-to-one ratio. I drank a ton of water and ate three main meals, then supplemented at the office or at home with a protein shake containing fruit, or a good-quality protein bar, a can of tuna in water, or a low-fat cottage cheese. My protein in my main meals involved salmon for the omega-3 fatty acids, and poultry, meat, and sushi at least twice a week. I never went more than an hour after any workout without ingesting protein to help heal the tissue damage associated with heavy training. My roomie at Palmer College of Chiropractic in the 1980's was Dr. Jay Manning, an expert in diagnosing and treating nutritional deficiencies using a technique called applied kinesiology. He checked and re-checked me and donated all the supplements I would need for training as well as stocked me up with vital nutrients for the ten weeks on the climb.

My nutritional plan worked. When I got on the plane at Green Airport in Warwick, RI, on March 23, 2008, I was a pumped and buff 173 pounds with less than nine percent body fat. However, when I returned to the same airport and kissed the ground and Rose in front of several television cameras in June, I was an embarrassingly emaciated 150 pencil-necked pounds without the strength to climb anything higher than the ramp to get into Rose's kitchen. The bathroom scale hadn't read that weight since I finished one of my marathons, badly dehydrated, while still in my teens. I can only imagine what I would have been like if I had not been as obsessive about weight training and nutrition.

As time grew short, Rose and I spent as much time as we could together. Her maddeningly frenetic time as a wedding and prom gown fashionista was nearly the time I was in Asia: March to June. Her business was so busy then that she traditionally would work to one or two a.m., sleep to five a.m., go for a power walk, then see clients and sew all day, sometimes seven days per week.

By my last day of work, Friday, March 22, 2008, Sharon and Joanne had Dr. Matt and the office well under control. My house was put to bed; best buddy Dana was paying my bills; Palmer, my obsessive-compulsive golden retriever, was comfortable in his home-away-from-home with the Culton family; Rose ramped up for her crazy time; so there was just one thing to do: party.

I hoped to have a private area at Ted's Montana Grill to converse with friends and family and eat bison steaks, but that's not what happened. It was loud and noisy and I didn't have much time to talk to buds like Bizil and Jay whom I didn't get to see much. I felt badly that I didn't have any quiet time with Kurt. Also, in the back of my mind was the phone call that Dana's eleven-year-old son Cameron had been diagnosed with type-one diabetes that day and would need insulin injections for the rest of his life. After dinner and goodbyes, the emotional parting as I dropped off Kurt, a cocktail with Rob and Jenny at Main Street Coffee, then I left for home with Rose.

As I held a sleeping Rose, I saw how her long, black hair accentuated her beautiful face perfectly on the white pillowcase. I smoothed her hair for the thousandth time and wondered what kind of extreme insanity I possessed that compelled me to leave her, leave Kurt and leave my work, travel around the world and maybe even get myself killed in the process. *Am I nuts or what?* These thoughts of dread and excitement made for a sleepless night until five a.m. when Rose drove me to the airport.

"Life only demands from you the strength you possess. Only one feat is possible: not to have run away."
— Dag Hammarskjold

A Warrior Loves His Craft

Chapter Three

"At last the ladder which had been built slowly, slowly,
one hope at a time, reached up to the clouds. And the
dreamer began to climb."

— unknown

What a multi-media, cultural, spiritual and sensual overload Kathmandu, Nepal provides; a constant cacophony of competing sounds, sights and smells. My second journey began on March 24, 2008, at Tribuhaven International Airport. After the casual customs rituals and fighting the screaming kids wanting to carry bags for tips, I hoisted my blood red Mammut trekking pack over my shoulders and comandeered a rickety cart to wheel my three huge duffels to the x-ray area. I pushed and coaxed the gargantuan bags through the machine, an x-ray contraption that doubtless wasn't on and probably hadn't worked in years.

Dispatch 28 March 2008 4500 feet

Safely in Nepal, and on time

All I can say is wow. That was the world's fastest year. Arriving in Kathmandu early yesterday morning and stepping out of the plane it was as if I had never left. The scent was the first clue, a mixture of wood smoke from cremations, diesel exhaust and decaying garbage. Don't get me wrong, I loved it. I roomed at Hotel Tibet with Chip Popovisciu. Great guy. We organized our gear in the wee hours as we will ship out to Lukla tomorrow at five a.m. Can't wait to get a move on this climb, though we haven't received our climbing permit yet! Gotta love politics. Later — Dr. Tim in Nepal.

Our greeters shooed away the attempted tip grabbers and placed the traditional welcome garland of pungent fresh marigolds around my neck. On the twenty-minute bus ride to the Hotel Tibet, I chatted with Ciprian "Chip" Popovisciu. Chip, originally from Romania, has a Ph.D. in physics, now lives in North Carolina and works for Cisco Systems, creating the next generation of the internet. With a long and lean endurance athlete build, Chip looked ready for Everest. He sported an eastern-block inability to pronounce the short vowels and some old-school muttonchops. He planned to meet up with his climbing buddy, Vance Cook, a software engineer and video-game entrepreneur from Salt Lake City. Vance's business claim to fame was creating the popular video game "Tiger Woods Golf."

The ornately carved wooden door and pungent potted plants greeted me at the Hotel Tibet entrance like old friends. Once inside, I felt downright homey amid the spotless dentate hardwood moldings, wool tapestries, Tibetan paintings and sculptures, especially when the staff greeted us as if we were, indeed, long lost family.

Chip and I were assigned to room together so we pushed, pulled and cajoled our worldly belongings into the rattle-trap elevator, poured ourselves into the room, and collapsed. We realized we were still in the manic phase of our jet lag so I suggested a beer at the tiny lobby bar. We ordered up two Mt. Everest beers, with labels bearing Tenzing Norgay striking that iconic summit pose from the pages of National Geographic nearly fifty-five years ago. We toasted to Sir Edmund Hillary, who sadly passed on in January 2008.

Chip knew this was my second Everest attempt and peppered me with questions which I happily, but carefully answered. I promised myself I would not be one of those self-proclaimed Everest experts, telling Nepal newbies what to do. I would not become boorish and, in fact, would only give suggestions if asked. Every group has a butthead. It wasn't going to be me.

Finally exhausted, we passed out for awhile, but I found myself awake and wired in the wee hours, tossing and turning. I didn't want to disturb Chip, but I really wanted to sort my gear. As soon as he made a sound, I asked him if I could turn on the light.

"Sure, can't sleep anyway."

My plan was to separate the two bags that would be carried by yaks to Base Camp and make sure there is nothing in them I would need for the next two weeks on the trek. My third bag would hold the paraphernalia for the trek that we could tap into each morning and night once it was offloaded from the yak.

After sorting bags we celebrated our first morning in Kathmandu by going to Mike's, an oasis of American breakfast with a Nepali twist.

Mike was an expatriate who arrived there in the early sixties while in the Peace Corp and never left, over the years becoming a respected member of the capital city. We Americans loved Mike's for its beautiful landscaped grounds, the best wait staff, the best coffee, exotic fruit juices and tastiest breakfast imaginable — breakfast is my favorite meal — all for 300 rupees (about $4). A Mike's meal provided significant improvement from the hotel breakfast of toast, barely palatable mini sausages, and rot-gut instant coffee.

Next, we hopped a cab to the Swambanunath Stupa (a.k.a. the Monkey Temple), a mixed place of worship for devotees of Buddhism and Hinduism. The temple sits high on a hill in the center of the teeming city and bustles at all hours. In 2007, Big Al and I, again jet-lagged, were there by four a.m. to watch the sun rise over the city. We carefully inched by dozens of semi-sleeping monkey families who violently screeched and bared their teeth when we got too close. We camped out and watched the first monks come out and do their chanting circumnavigations of the centerpiece five-story-high white-domed stupa while the monkeys acrobatically climbed, hand over hand, up the prayer flags while catching moths to eat. That morning, Buddhist and Hindu stood shoulder to shoulder peacefully worshiping.

Chip and I saw it again that morning: two of the world's major religions co-existing without fringe extremists killing each other in a twisted rationalization of religious doctrine. The rest of the world should take careful note.

On our way back to the hotel we saw pickup trucks laden with Maoist campaign people handing out leaflets, blaring political slogans over PA systems and clogging the roads by the busy market areas. It was election time in Nepal. The word was that people were disillusioned with King Gyanendra, head of the monarchy that had run Nepal for over 240 years. Many people were starting to become enamored with the Maoists, a violent communist political group, who seemed to have a shot to win in the April 14th elections. We would be climbing Everest on that date. Presumably, after the summit, we could return to the capital and there could be a new government in Nepal after a quarter of a millennium.

We went back to the hotel for a dead-to-the-world sleep until a phone call told us we were late for a mandatory five p.m. team meeting. There must have been thirty-five folks present, all staring at us, the last to arrive. I gave Ang Jangbu a fond shake and a man-hug to Mark Tucker. Eric Simonson had started the introductions so I found a seat and mouthed my silent greetings to Casey Grom, Mike Hamill, and

Dave Hahn, all guides, and Joe Yanuzzi, an attorney from Philadelphia, a climber I had met climbing in North Conway, NH.

The trekking team of ten was there, two of whom Jim and Kate Swetnam, were on the Mt.Kilimanjaro climb with buddy Bob Degregorio and myself in 1999. I can remember on summit day of that great African continental high point, Kate saying "This is the trip of a lifetime" I responded, *It's only the trip of a lifetime until the next one.* It was great to see them. On the ensuing trek we swapped stories of the 19,340 foot climb and the safari afterward.

At the meeting, I found out that the climb team and the trek team would share the trail to Base Camp where the trek team would stay a day or two and beat a hasty retreat while we summit hopefuls would toil and fret our way to the summit and back for an additional month to six weeks.

Then we went back to our room and the strategy for final prep: leave one small bag of street clothes and shoes at the hotel for our return; three duffels to fly, two of which I would be reunited with in Base Camp; one for the trek which I would have access to morning and night, each day to be carried by a porter or yak; and my trusty backpack which I would, of course, carry with me on the plane and daily on the trek. I charged up all the batteries I could in the hotel bathroom — satellite phone, hand held computer, Canon high-definition movie camera, iPod, and both trek and climbing Canon cameras. Before bed, I applied padlocks to my three huge duffels and dropped off easily to sleep.

Going to Lukla the next morning, I sighted a yeti! Actually, we all did as we boarded our flights on Yeti Air. Everyone wants to see the mythical abominable snowman but the Sherpa lore has it that, if you actually catch a glimpse of the famously shy beast, you will die within the following twenty-four hours. Yeti Air was close enough for me.

On the hour-long flight in the dual-propped twenty person plane, we nearly sat on the laps of the two pilots, cradling our packs on our laps, while the solitary, demure flight attendant handed out hard candy and cotton balls for our ears. The engines' drone made conversation impossible, but I saw looks of excited expectancy and apprehension in my fellow mountaineers. As we flew higher, I remembered when buddy Rob Scott and I climbed Denali in 2004, our glacier pilot Jay Hudson said as we took off, "Grab your testicles and your spectacles and hang on!" It was a toss-up as to which of the two flying experiences was the most exciting.

For the first twenty minutes of the flight we were above the hazy terrain of cultivated, increasingly mountainous, foothills which led, in the next twenty minutes, to higher and more remote precipices and impossibly deep chasms, before we finally caught site of the tiny postage stamp of an airfield at Lukla 9,000 feet. The short runway ran uphill after landing, to slow the planes as they landed. Just before smashing into the forty-foot-high vertical rock buttress at the end, the pilot took a hard ninety degree right while reversing engines, pulling to a stop seconds later at the airport's single building. (During the fall trekking season, a group of twenty German tourists and their pilots died when, in a bit of fog, the fence had been clipped by the plane's rear wheels upon touchdown.) We screeched to a stop, and chaos erupted as baggage handlers threw our gear out of the plane's storage and started to reload before we even uncoiled ourselves from our seatbelts.

Walking off the field, I warmly greeted Passang Rinjing, Big Al's Sherpa from his successful Everest 2007 climb. We were a little team of four within the bigger team of twenty western climbers and twenty Sherpas that year. Passang is not only a summit climber but would make a few extra double-dipping bucks this year helping our team all the way to Base Camp with cooking and carrying.

Soon we shouldered our packs and took our first steps on the trek through the muddy main street of downtown Lukla. Our elevation was 9,000 feet, already 3,000 feet above the highest point in the Northeast United States. After all the hours sitting on planes it felt great to be physically active. The weight of my backpack, the rhythm of striding along the trail, even the challenge of breathing the thinner air all made the mission real, tangible. After all the preparation, I'd finally begun.

Our destination for the day was Phak-Ding, a small hamlet on the Dudh Khosi, or Milk River, so named because of its grey silt from the grinding glaciers of the high mountains ahead. The terrain reminded me of those National Geographic photos I had studied as a kid. I'd looked at those pictures and wondered who lived in those places, what kind of lives they led. And now there I was hiking through those very pictures. I could reach out and touch the beautiful colors of the brightly painted teahouses and the picture-perfect manicured farms surrounded by ornately carved Mani stones and prayer wheel buildings, all in the shadow of huge Himalayan peaks. I heard the constant roar of the river below us.

The trek provided ample opportunity to gather good karma, by passing the aforementioned mani stones (huge boulders with carved prayers usually painted in blue or white) on the left, and spinning prayer wheels, with the right hand only, thank you.

At that stage of the trek we were an amorphous, spread-out group of thirty two. Sherpa helpers, porters and yak drivers came and went throughout the day as our group either plodded the dusty trail or passed out on a rest and acclimatization day. Our team included the eleven self-guided climbers plus Dean Smith, Jaroslaw Hawrylewicz and Nicole and Greg Messner, whose guides, Justin Merle and Dave Hahn, waited for our permits back in Kathmandu. There were also our trekking team and our IMG management team of Mark Tucker, Ang Jangbu and Lobsang Sherpa joined by IMG owner Eric Simonson who hiked with us until Namche Bazaar.

There was constant banter as we all tried to sort out who was climbing and who was trekking. Conversation came to an end, however, when we tackled steep ascents of the many spectacular gorges, the first real test of our unacclimatized lungs. Simply bending over to tie my shoes, at high altitude, evoked the same heart and respiration rate increases that my Rhode Island workouts provided. The ascents of steep gorges on the hike to Base Camp elicited pulmonary yammering that was scary fast. Our lungs were still virgin territory for the low oxygen levels and it would be weeks before we could hike even a moderate hill without sucking wind like a two-pack-a-day smoker.

I planned to hang in the middle of the pack for the trek and take it easy, because I never acclimatize particularly fast and this was not a race. People drifted up-trail and down; there was always someone interesting to talk to or, if I wanted to be alone, there was plenty of time for that, too. I found myself looking more closely at my surroundings this year than last and was constantly amazed at the beauty of the land, the architecture and the people. I believed it was because I had "accepted" the climb to come. My goal was clear, so I could enjoy the road and be in the moment.

There were two women on the climbing team and two on the trekking team, about average in climbing expeditions. It must be a drag for the ladies to be surrounded by all these boisterous, often obnoxious, alpha-males for eight to ten weeks, but they all seemed to be cheerfully resilient, even Val Hovland, the only woman who came unaccompanied by a husband. Eventually both Val and Nicole summited in 2008, while ten of the twenty one guys from our group got to the top.

Soon the routine of the trek to Base Camp was set. Each afternoon our Sherpa helpers bolted ahead of the group to set up camp at the next village. They set up our tents, put a sleeping pad in each, and started to prepare dinner in the nearest teahouse. As we unacclimatized hurtin' hombres trickled into camp at different times, the trick for each of us was to find the yak carrying our own duffel bag, and drag the bugger to the correct tent (the duffel was dragged ... not the yak).

The window of time between hiking and dinner, offered the opportunity to take a nap or read a bit before gathering in the dining room to attack mugs of Sherpa tea or hot lemon in front of the yak dung stove. *Hydrate or die* became my mantra throughout each day on the trail, and especially at each meal, as fluids thin the blood and aid acclimatization.

The trail began to demand more of our attention through steep intense climbs and precipitous downclimbs, all while dodging porters, yak trains and multitudes of yak patties on the heavily trodden four-foot-wide rock and sand track. Centuries of feet and yak hooves have worn the rock walkway but eroded areas are well maintained with fresh-hewn rock and mortar with labor supplied by masons compensated by donations placed in a brightly painted blue wooden box constructed for that purpose. Such care was critical because maintenance of this centuries-old path is a key to Nepal's economy. There are no roads to Base Camp or to any of the surrounding mountains. This trail was it, where all those climbers, trekkers and adventure seekers must place their kicks. It's not Route 66; only a primitive dirt path, albeit one of prime importance for the Khumbu Valley. These trails have never seen a wheeled vehicle, not even a mountain bike, as the terrain is simply too rugged for anything other than foot or hoof. Everything in the Khumbu, from beer to buildings, was brought here either on someone's back or on someone's yak.

While I'm on the subject, in Phak-Ding and upward to Pangboche, the yaks are actually crossbreeds of cattle and yaks called zopkios, but above that are the serious real deal yaks. Essentially, cows on steroids, yaks are thick, hairy outrageously strong. They are considered important members of the Sherpa's family, usually decorated with prayer flags and other articles of Buddhist worship. Yaks are bought and sold and can be used to rent out to treks or expeditions, for food and even for fuel. No wonder they are important to Sherpas.

The yak dung is gathered in baskets, dried, mixed with sawdust and kerosene, and burned for heat and cooking. After a lifetime of breathing the particulate matter resulting from the burning of yak poop, it's no wonder Sherpas' life expectancy in the Khumbu is fifty-five or younger, usually due to pulmonary disease.

This path is a cash cow (or cash yak) for the locals as well as the country of Nepal since tourism, and most specifically trekking, brings in much needed bucks for this poorest of poor economies. Each Everest climber pays a $10,000 fee to the Kingdom of Nepal for the permit just to make the attempt, but that's not the bulk of the tourism dollar. It is the infrastructure of goods and services surrounding the hiking and climbing visitors that brings relative wealth.

We woke the next morning in the hamlet of Phak-Ding and prepared to advance up the famously long, steep and painful Namche Hill to the cultural and social hub of the Khumbu valley: Namche Bazaar (11,000 feet) where we would acclimatize for two additional days. On the way, we passed tiny villages with excellent names: Ghat gives way to Nurning which leads to Dukdingma followed by Zam-Fute and Monjo, and up the trail is one of my all-time favorites: Thumbug. Making a strong showing for most fun name in the Khumbu Valley — Phunki-Tenga.

The "Hill" was where I plugged the iPod to my brain, clicked into my Namche playlist and trudged upward for two hours on nature's step-mill, fueled by energy gel and Neil Young. (Energy gel, my brand was called GU, is a small single-serving squeeze pouch of nutrients, used commonly by endurance athletes.) I felt physically well, and people commented on how strong and focused I seemed; quite different from 2007, when I never seemed to get my groove on. No matter how studly you feel and appear, there's no getting around it, these steep up-hills really hurt. I just went slowly and steadily and rest-stepped whenever possible.

The rest-step is a climbing technique I learned on Mt. Rainier. The rest-step allows you to climb brutally steep hills relatively comfortably, albeit slowly, even with monumental pack weights. The idea was to quickly snap your rear leg onto a locked position so your weight was on the bone structure and not on the musculature for a half-second or so before throwing the opposite leg forward.

There are various additional tricks to becoming very efficient in rest-stepping, like a slight forward lean to the body's trunk before becoming upright once that rear leg is locked shut. On the Namche hill, as on all hills to come, I practiced my technique so when I got to the mother of all hills on summit day, I would have it wired into my central nervous system like Tiger hitting a nine-iron.

We all have differing speeds of hiking, and, although I planned to be in the middle, I found myself at or near the front group the entire trek. That fast hiking group included Crazy Joe Yanuzzi (so named by yours truly because he's quiet and can go for hours without saying a word), Chip, Vance, Scott Parazynski, a NASA astronaut with multiple space shuttle flights and spacewalks to his credit, and Adam Janikowski, an investment professional from Canada who was Scott's climbing partner. The trekkers, as you might expect, were usually much slower but seemed to be doing OK. Fast, slow or in between, everyone on the team was eventually visited by a variety of the normal symptoms for third-world high altitude expeditions: fatigue, nausea, colds, diarrhea, loss of appetite and headaches.

Upon reaching Namche we started International Mountain Guide's cultural habit of grabbing the highest camp, or, in this case, teahouse, available. It's a righteous plan on the mountain as you have fewer hours to go to the next checkpoint, but getting to the teahouse just plain hurts. Plodding to the Sherpa Lodge at the uppermost rim of the Namche amphitheatre, up one cobblestone at a time with heaving lungs, was the first place to bow to the god of suffering on this trip. I knew it wouldn't nearly be the last.

In addition to the deep musculo-skeletal dull ache that impacted my every panting step with a rhythmic pain-fest, I had the added embarrassment of being a member of the slowest group there. Local Sherpa shopkeepers, lodge workers, even the yaks and chickens scurried about at a normal pace. Other trekking groups, staying at the lodge at this altitude for at least a day longer than we, moved with a great deal more speed than did our "fast" group. We resigned ourselves to a simple truth — at each new altitude we were broken men and women until the myriad physiological miracles took place and we acclimatized.

And now for some political news, or at least some political controversies. I'll take a little time to explain it here, just to show you that, no matter how much each of us trained or planned, events that had little to do with our team stood directly in our path to Everest. The head cheese of International Mountain Guides, Eric Simonson, who, along with Phil Erschler and Geo Dunn, formed the guide business in the 1980s, accompanied us, as he did in 2007, as far as Namche. Eric is an Everest summiter but was best known for organizing the expeditions that found George Leigh Mallory's body on Everest's north side in 1999. Controversy remains that Mallory and Sandy Ervine could have been Everest's first summiters in the 1920s. Most experts agree, however, that there was little chance that the duo got to the top before meeting their demise on descent.

Eric and I got off on the wrong foot when he called me four days before leaving for Nepal in 2007, requesting that I redo my entire expedition application, which I had sent in eight months before. I refused. I simply had too much to do. Besides, I reasoned … that job should have been completed well before we were about to leave. Maybe as a result of our disagreement, we were a tad aloof with each other when we met in Kathmandu. Then he got peeved at me (and Al) again because in the wee hours, while camped next to Eric, Al and I talked and giggled like schoolgirls and kept him awake.

The more serious issue between us happened while I was in Base Camp and Eric was 7,000 miles away in Seattle. (It seems no distance is great enough, nor mountain high enough to keep me from pissing people off.) The brouhaha began because I had been sending dispatches to a blog on my web site that several hundred people and media outlets were following. The "Eric Rule" was, "no communicating any information about anybody other than yourself." This rule was instituted as a result of the 2006 IMG expedition when two team members had blogged about a climbing death on the mountain before the Kingdom of Nepal had announced it, as is customary. As sure as bodies roll downhill, the European family of the deceased began calling Eric for answers he could not give from such distance.

Leave it to little old me to add, the very next year, to this veritable shit-storm of controversy by my dispatches. On April 2, 2007, Eric, through Base Camp consigliore Mark Tucker, in front of the entire team at dinner, threatened to kick me off the team. Here, verbatim were the offending words from my satellite transmission that day: "The trek in (to Base Camp) was NOT easy. Two people had to quit on the way and virtually one hundred percent had some health issue from GI issues, to altitude, to infections of all sorts. Luanne Freer, a volunteer MD, even had to do minor surgery on one of us."

Stupidly, I thought this passage innocuous at the time, but I quickly realized upon inspection I wasn't being anonymous at all, but had, like a dope, included everyone on the team. Eric could have been inundated with endless whining relatives hungry for info since "everyone" was sick. Worse, the staff at Explorers Web, the most influential of Everest web sites, ran that snippet in their daily report, sharing it with a wider world — and gave me credit. *Great.*

I was horrified at what I had done and terrified that Simo would follow through on his threat to give me the heave-ho from the climbing team. How would I repay my sponsors, two of whom had come up with $20,000 each for my climb? I felt the same shame as when I was caught red-handed by Mrs. Leibert using salty words in the second grade. I apologized to Tuck and the whole team publicly and Luanne privately the next day at the Puja ceremony. Eventually it all blew over. *Whew!*

Even though all was forgiven and in 2008 we got along swimmingly on a personal level, this year's "Chinese situation" brought Eric to an understandably high level of stress.

Eric painted the picture on IMG's Everest blog on March 21, 2008. "I have said before that each year is different when it comes to Everest, and 2008 is shaping up to be no exception! Just when we were celebrating the end of civil war in Nepal and the prospects of nationwide elections this spring, it seems that world events conspire to make the Everest season unpredictable. The recent instability in Tibet and the diplomatic pressure that the Chinese have put on Nepal to close the south side of Everest makes us remember that it is not just the weather, avalanches and ice we struggle with, but also government and politics. Knock on wood, it now looks like we will get our Everest permits, with some conditions — we will likely have to come down while the Chinese are summiting with the Olympic torch from the north side. The exact details will be forthcoming and we will keep everyone updated on this."

So, in addition to the usual logistics of sending three MI-17 helicopter charters to Shyangboche with over 22,000 pounds of food, fuel and supplies to be re-packed onto six hundred and fifty yak loads and sent to Base Camp, and packing and re-packing the oxygen shipment from Kathmandu, it sufficed to say that Eric had a few things on his mind.

Even before leaving the United States, rumors abounded online and through e-mails about just what we climbers would face because of Chinese restrictions. Eric Simonson called on Crazy Joe, a skilled Philadelphia lawyer and strong-as-hell climber, to draft a document for all of us to sign at a team meeting at The Sherpa Lodge. The document said we agreed to toe the line on whatever rule the Chinese came up with. We don't sign? We go home, simple as that. Simonson's business was on the line there. If one of us summited and unfurled a "Free Tibet" flag, ruining China's propaganda party with the Olympic flame, Eric could lose his Nepal guiding privileges — a disaster for him, as Everest is the crown jewel of his company's focus.

Eric passed out copies of the document and we went through it, line by line, for two hours, debating, dissecting, even though none of us (including Eric) yet had a clue what specifics the Chinese would be demanding. OK, so they say we can't climb when the Chinese are on their summit attempt and we can't have any communication with the outside world, or film anything without "approval" whatever that meant. Obviously, they didn't want even the possibility of negative news.

Jim Harter, a climber from California, who made his fortune in gas, oil and real estate, finally said, "I just don't think I can sign this."

Simo retorted, "No problem. You can leave right now."

The proverbial yak poop hit the fan with angry outbursts from all sides — except from me. I signed the document without blinking, and Eric Simonson went home to Seattle.

A team acclimatization hike was scheduled for the next day which I deferred to get to a cyber-café (yes, even in the mountains of Nepal). I had Joe Bannister, my web guy in Rhode Island, scrub my dispatches, both past and present for any stray comment that might inflame the Chinese, cause World War Three, or, worst of all, keep me from climbing Mt. Everest. Just in case, I also contacted Tom Sjogren at Explorers Web, imploring him not to print anything I had written — past or present. I recalled some choice dispatches in 2007 in which I opined politically about the Chinese invasion and subsequent annexation of Tibet in 1950, and the resultant abuses still going on today.

On his web site, Tom is very committed to bringing past and present abuses to the public. (For example, he reported that in Cho Oyu Base Camp, Chinese soldiers shot and killed nuns and children who were trying to escape religious and personal persecution by going over the high mountainous pass of Nangpa La to Nepal.) On my climb, however, I would not fight that battle. I was there to climb Everest and return safely. After nearly getting the boot from the 2007 adventure in blogging, I just wanted to get my permit and climb on — without controversy.

Mark Tucker pretty much stayed out of the arguing at the meeting and shrugged apologetically when we made eye contact post meeting. Smoothly professional, he had a wonderful mix of human understanding, competency in climbing — a seven summiter, including Everest in 1990 on the Peace Climb — and innate management skills. In 2007 I saw him do a masterful job of diffusing two potential dust-ups at Base Camp. One involved two overly testosteroned policemen trekking in with us who nearly came to blows. The other involved a notable climbing guide who came to Tuck to mediate after an altercation in the icefall. Tuck's sincere question, "How can I help?" worked perfectly in those situations and I marveled at its simplicity and power. Every team on Everest came to Tuck for advice and he truly embodied the moniker of "Mayor of Base Camp." Other than his penchant for unbridled wagering in non-stop dining tent poker games, he was my kind of climbing CEO.

The days and villages meandered by like silt in the Dudh Khosi river: hike a little, rest a little, rest a little more, get to a higher elevation and let the body acclimatize, drink and pee twenty-four-seven to increase red blood cell production and carry more oxygen to our starved tissue, eat everything in sight, even when not hungry, spin some prayer wheels, see a view that you just can't believe exists in nature, repeat and repeat again.

"Traveling teaches you as much about the places you leave behind as it does the place you are visiting."
— Paul Watkins

At home we deal with hygiene and the call of nature as just part of the day. We take the opportunity for a shower or excretion for granted. Just something that has to be done. Not so out here. Every pee or poop was a strategic act; planned, thought out, an unwelcome adventure. And showers? More mythical than real.

By the fifth day out, I felt desperate for a shower. My hair became so greasy and my odor so bad, I really needed to de-louse. But it wasn't going to happen. Pee and poo? There was no putting those off — at least not for long. But there are certain pieces of equipment that can help. Such a device was my half-gallon collapsible pee bottle, the envy of my team. Light, space saving, with huge capacity and a large mouth opening for rolling over and peeing while still in the tent or the tea-house, kind of like having a bedpan in the hospital, but in this case, a luxury. There was no need to unzip a warm sleeping bag, put on boots or struggle to get out of the tent because you've waited until the last possible second to wizz, hoping you don't freeze your fingers and a certain delicate body part which must be left uncovered to do its work.

More than once, I filled that gargantuan vessel to the brim before dumping it among the rocks next morning. Of course, the pee bottle didn't help with the pooping. For that we had to exit the tent in parka and headlamp to pick our way carefully around tent stakes and lines to the temporary communal outhouse tent specially constructed by our Sherpa team. Peeing is one thing. You can always find an isolated spot. But an outhouse? We all had to use the same one. Sometimes one after the other. No leisurely reading of the paper here. No flush, either, the accumulation of the previous users was piled beneath us for all to smell.

So it didn't help that there always seems to be someone with a gastro-intestinal problem who perfumed the little outhouse with a fragrance that even overwhelmed the cold. Above Base Camp, in Camp One and Camp Three, a poop hole was dug and marked well. In Camp Two, otherwise known as Advanced Base Camp, the Sherpa team will put a small tent over the rocks together with a can and plastic bag liner. People will take turns on the really gross job of emptying that quite nasty bag into a crevasse. When I see pictures of jubilant climbers summiting Everest, I know they are probably thinking, "In a few more days I'll be able to take a shower! I'll be able to take a crap in a toilet!"

On the trek to Base Camp, I tried to remember people's names, where they were from, who was trekking and who was climbing, a tough task considering we had team members from Jamaica, Poland, Romania, Canada, Taiwan, and, of course, the United States. One guy I got to know, Willi, a radiologist from New York City, and originally from Korea did not enjoy his first foray into trekking. He paid the $6,500 for the trip (a lower fee for trekkers), picked up all the required gear for at least another $2,000, took three weeks' leave from his job in a New York City hospital — and landed smack dab in misery.

Willi just wasn't prepared physically or mentally for the daily grind of hiking up seriously big hills with a thirty pound pack on his back, then sleeping on the ground with a tent-mate (Gary, our trek M.D.) who snored like a slowly choking goat. Things went from bad to worse for poor Willi when altitude sickness and gastro-intestinal disturbances added to his stew of unhappiness. Nobody makes it through weeks in the Himalayas unscathed from various and sundry maladies, but the Everest Base Camp trek was not the place to make your debut into outdoor adventure.

Third-world hygiene and relative close proximity of team members make it imperative to be constantly vigilant of the state of your stomach. I learned the hard way in 2007 to Purel my hands almost every time I touched anything public, like a doorknob or a Fanta bottle. Willi, or any of us, could become contaminated from people's hands or a yak's back or just from whatever blew around in the air.

At other times, we just had to trust the western hygienic food prep training of our group and in the odd teahouse where we stopped for a bite. But even then we learned to pass plates to each other with our thumbs *under* the plate, to minimize risk of nastiness transmission. We met the inevitable mini-epidemic at Dingboche at 14,000 feet, but, by quarantining myself out of the tent and into a local teahouse, I was able to dodge that bullet. I felt glad to escape from the tent I shared with Chip for a day or two while the poor guy sorted out his malaise. Every time he opened his mouth his sulfur-laden breathe smelled like rapidly decaying eggs.

Of course, at this stage of the game we all smelled about the same after six days on the trail and that same tell-tale scent remained for the entire expedition, even if we had the good fortune to have an occasional solar-powered luke-warm shower. In reality, we all smelled like a can of smashed assholes, it's just that we were no longer terribly offended by it.

Blessed for Everest 3/31/08

Yesterday was a cool day! We left the town of Namche and had some up and down climbing for two hours before an early lunch, then bang…big long grind of an uphill to Tengboche and its famous monastery. We lazed a bit, then camped twenty minutes down trail in a yak pasture in Deboche. We were up early today because we had a meeting with the the Rinpoche of Tengboche Monastery. We presented him with kata scarves and donations, and we each received a blessing as he placed the scarves, one by one around our necks. (Rinpoche means reincarnated lama.) Several of us hiked up the hill a second time later in the day for a service (and a slice of cake at a small bakery). We are about 12,000 feet and going to 14,000 feet tomorrow. Hope all is well at home.   Dr. Tim

---

Dispatch

Blessing Bound 4/1/08

Hello from Deboche (fifteen minutes and a little downhill from Tengboche Monastery). We are camped at about 12,000 feet in a beautiful spot. I saw my first view of Everest today… just as momentous as last year. Tomorrow is a rest and acclimatization day and it looks like we will get a blessing from the Lama at the monastery. I am really excited because he was not in last year. I am feeling quite strong and fit and taking great care of my throat by breathing through a cloth buff and sucking lozenges. It seems I will be able to dispatch a little longer. Over and out. Tim

---

Dugla for lunch and Lobuche for dinner was the order of the day. The former is a village consisting of three buildings and an outhouse. Dugla is the terminus of a confluence of trails from Dingboche and

Pheriche. Its location is at a very questionable, wobbly yak bridge, across a roaring patch of violently crashing water from glaciers a three day hike away. Our world changed from lush farmland to scrub hill-sides, to above-timber-line yak grass savannas, and was now giving way to rock broken into all shapes and sizes. The roaring rivers swollen with glaciel-melt were our constant companions, and their rocky banks let us know in no uncertain terms that we were nearing the nexus of their creation: the cirque of our world's greatest mountains, including the one undisputed greatest of them all.

An hour long gut-busting uphill stretch involving countless rocky switchbacks in increasing wind and cold, brought us to the crest of a ridge. In clear weather, it was made visible miles away by thousands of colorful prayer flags and shredded kata scarves whipping about "chortens," areas of contemplation and tribute to all the Himalayan climbers who have died in the mountains.

We all stopped and sat in silence taking in the significance of the multitudes of these stone chortens or shrines; each one erected in honor of a deceased climber.

"A climb is always implicative...it points us out to ourselves."
— **Pat Ament**

Here is the dispatch I sent when I first came upon this place, a year earlier.

Dispatch 3/31/07 15,500 feet

In Memoriam

Many people have read *Into Thin Air* by Jon Krakauer and are, therefore, familiar with the tragedy that unfolded in the Everest climbing season of 1996.

It was a somber feeling when we climbed a ridge and found ourselves in the memorial for climbers who had lost their lives in the Himalayas. "Chortens" are stone memorials standing two to twelve feet high, and there were a hundred or so. Rob Hall, Babu Chirii Sherpa, Yasuko Namba, Scott Fischer and Alex Lowe were some of the notables. The lesson for me is to be reverent and humble and to work with nature and not force anything. The summit and safe return is the objective but if that seems doubtful I will opt for the safe return. Over and out, — Dr. Tim

---

I sat listening once again to the wind snap at the prayer flags and looked over those cold stones, the reminders of what happened to healthy, strong young men and women skilled in the ways of the mountains, I realized that none of them expected to die as they trekked up to Base Camp, passing this very spot. But die they did.

How do you wrap yourself around the idea of death in relation to living your dream or following your mission? I must admit, after my previous Everest experience, I was even more attentive to this reality: through 2008, two hundred and ten climbers had died on Mt. Everest. Of these, one hundred and twenty bodies remained uncovered on the upper ramparts. They all had missions on Everest just like me. Craig John told me that while involved in a rescue high on Everest in 1994, "I gained an understanding of how and why people die up there. When you stop up there it would be so easy to not get started again. It feels so good to stop — almost euphoric — to not move."

I could die up there, too. It's a crap shoot. Yet I remained confident in my ability to make good decisions when the chips were down. My experience in 2007 when I decided to turn my tail around, put it between my legs and go home was a good example. Good decisions eliminate a high percentage of death on The Big E. The human error or "subjective hazard" factor in climbing defines such scenarios as continuing to climb in bad weather or when sick or exhausted. I was pretty confident in my ability to minimize those risks. The big unknown for me was how my brain and lungs would do in the death zone above 25,000 feet. *Will my brain swell with cerebral edema, rendering my decision making, agility, and balance roughly the same as a drunk driver flunking a sobriety test?* I didn't know. Nobody does. Even if you have summited an 8,000 meter peak before and performed well, there is no guarantee that you won't get an altitude-related life-threatening disease on the next climb. There are fourteen 8000 meter (26,000 feet) mountains in the world, and all are in the Himalayan Range in Nepal, Tibet or Pakistan.

Beyond subjective hazards there was the more pesky issue of objective hazards: those circumstances over which you have no control — avalanches, rock fall on the Lhotse Face, icefall collapse, the situations that can kill you, the situations that, when you are in your tent alone, got in your head, and stayed there all night, especially when you were sick or exhausted.

In 2007, Al and I stood somberly in the Western Cwm (a cwm is a Scottish term meaning "valley" and here refers to the real estate between Camp One and Camp Two at 21,500 feet) as a dead Sherpa climber's body was trucked down the snow slope in a makeshift sled from the base of the Lhotse Face. He evidently had been hit by one of the madly careening rocks sailing off the mountain thousands of feet up. He probably never saw it coming, and it crushed his skull, killing him instantly. Days later, two Koreans were killed when their tent was avalanched off the Southwest Face behind our Camp Two. Shortly after that, an entire rope team of four Nepalis (including the first Nepali woman to summit Everest) fell to their deaths on the Lhotse Face, leaving red streaks in the snow and ice for thousands of feet.

These were some of the things on my mind as I sat on the cold stone seats on Chorten Ridge. The increasing wind chilled me into putting on my wind layer. I couldn't help but wonder if some in our group were marching to their deaths. I wondered if my teammates regarded death as a possibility, however small, or would they do everything in their power to deny death? One by one they crested the hill and nervously milled about. We were all somber and reverent, spoke little, took a few pictures and read the brass plaques. Everest confronted us here in all its cold reality. After twenty minutes or so I shouldered my pack and moved on, alone with my thoughts.

"You cannot run away from a weakness; you must sometimes fight it out or perish; and if that is so, why not now, and where you stand."
— Robert Louis Stevenson

Lobuche is a cute little berg of five or six stone houses nestled under its namesake mountain with a meandering stream running through it and some ponies and yaks wandering about. I think it got a bum rap in *Into Thin Air* as Krakauer described it as a fetid, open sewer. Granted, we didn't pitch our tents in town but in the suburbia of the yak pastures that surrounded this tiny village.

We had a rest day in Lobuche so Vance, Chip and I took a little acclimatization hike on the grassy slopes above the village. We picked our way around leisurely, and gazed at the amazing scenes playing out endlessly in all directions: soaring jagged peaks with massive ice-laden shoulders; down valley, great green valleys with centuries-old pastoral farming scenes; up trail to the west of us, the jumbled stone and ice floor of the terminal snout of the Khumbu glacier emitted from Sagermatha herself, and underneath, beginning in trickle and ending in torrent: the Dudh Khosi River.

Despite the beauty around us, I needed some basic comforts by then. *One more night to Base Camp, to Wheat Thins,*

I told myself. At this point I couldn't wait to delve into my large duffel bags with my own space to put them in. The constant set-up and take down of gear had gotten seriously old. I smelled like an old yak and I needed to delouse as best I could once we reached what would be our home for the bulk of the next two months: 17,300 foot Base Camp.

The last way station before Base was Gorak Shep (Dead Raven) at 16,800 feet, a cluster of three or four stone teahouses. It sat next to a vast dried lake bed and at the foot of the trekking peak, Kala Patthar,18,500 feet (a trekking peak is one that demands little or no technical climbing skill — basically a hike up a long trail.). Gorak Shep was where some of the most dramatic photos of Mt. Everest have been taken. Take a picture there as the sun sets on its massive bulk and you would swear that the mountain was molten.

We decided to get rooms at Ang Tsering's teahouse instead of pitching the tents. I was thrilled until I saw the room: so small that Crazy Joe and I couldn't stand or turn around at all with our debris on the floor. As soon as the sun went down, it became shockingly cold, as if we were in a meat cooler, only way smaller. To add to the fun and games, turning over in bed was a major production as the sleeping platforms were maybe six feet in length and two feet wide. Getting out of bed to dump the pee bottle was a near impossibility, so I held off as long as possible. To top it off, I had an altitude-induced doozie of a headache with severe nausea and nary a chiropractor in sight.

I was upright at five a.m. and still feeling like a train wreck, packed my duffel and dragged it outside into the frozen air, where I suddenly realized it was much warmer than in our miniscule stone-enclosed bedroom. *What is this, a subterfuge of physics?*

Vance, Chip, Crazy Joe, Mingma Sherpa, and I got an early jump and headed for Base Camp. The last stretch of trail to Base Camp started at the dry lake bed at the foot of Kala Pattar and skirted the huge lateral moraine over which we had climbed on the previous day's hike out of Lobuche. The ice floes of the Khumbu glacier have slowly built up huge piles of stone debris over the years, and they hovered over us on both sides of the trail. The stone rip-rap was elevated at least two-hundred feet above us in places. We hiked on an increasingly flattened plateau of broken rock mixed with ice, giving a characteristic turquoise hue to pools of melt water that formed and dissolved daily on the surface of the moving glacier.

The five of us followed the trail on the ridge of the left lateral moraine for the first hour, and then passed what I consider a potentially dangerous area. About fifty yards above us in an eroding cliff loomed huge boulders — half in and half out of the earth. Below us, having fallen and broken into countless pieces, were the remnants of splintered rock. This whole area was in constant transition. It's only a matter of time before some of these huge crowning boulders, the size of Chevy Suburbans, gave birth in a hail of sparks and splintered stone, and wiped out whatever yaks or people were below. Needless to say, I kept a constant wary eye upward in this area with a plan that if a runaway boulder came at me I would wait until the last possible second and sprint or dive to either side to dodge the rock-fall. If the falling stones were small and unavoidable, I'd turn and take the hit on my pack rather than my person (a little trick I had learned on Mt. Rainier). Each time through this shooting gallery I breathed a sigh of relief as we turned onto the glacier proper and safety.

I realized in how much better shape I was than last year as we blazed into Base Camp in two hours. In ten minutes, we saw the first colorful tents already festooned with thousands of prayer flags perched among huge gray stones.

Our Sherpa team had been hard at work for two weeks leveling tent platforms from the ice and rock and placing small stones so water wouldn't collect in the inevitable melting that happens as the season goes on. In addition to our individual smaller tent platforms, it took many Sherpas days to hack their way through the ice with steel bars, shovels and old ice axes to level large tent platforms for the communications tent, the two huge dining tents, the cook tent and the storage (movie night) tent. Despite the solid ice the Sherpas encountered, the ice floe beneath Base Camp was in continuous flux; an actual river ran beneath us. I remembered that last year, at night, I could often hear the water running beneath my sleeping bag as if someone had left a faucet on. That and the constant cracking of ice told us that Base Camp surfaces were always changing, so each team must carve out its own level spaces every year.

We wound our way through the under-construction tent city and around a yak or two and I showed Joe where Hillary and Tenzing's Base Camp was placed in the first ascent year of 1953. Then, Mingma proudly led us onto the steps of a mini-amphitheatre of stone steps that the Sherpas had somehow man-handled into place. Before we could extricate ourselves from our pack straps, we were clapped on the back by rowdy, friendly-faced Sherpas, who had poured out to greet us, one of whom pushed a mug of steaming lemon tea into my hands.

Jaroslaw said one day in camp, "Failing? I'm not worried about making the summit. I'm worried about not making the summit. Being here for seventy days, going through all the blood, sweat and tears and not making the summit would be an absolute disaster." He did make it. But if he hadn't, I wonder what he'd think of those seventy days. Sounds as if they would have been a waste of his time, a sentence he had to serve so he could get to the top.

"When you are facing in the right direction, keep putting one foot in front of the other."
— **Phinjo Sherpa**

Jaroslaw was a cool guy and a great teammate (and it was great fun to bust his beans) but I had a different take. I saw the fruits of a seventy day expedition in the enjoyment of everything you can possibly experience. That's a lesson I took from both years in Nepal. The lesson started on the long hike to Base Camp, where trekkers and climbers all got to know each other, share the environment and scenery so few others in the world are privileged to be part of, eat hot meals, crawl into sleeping bags comfortably spent, and sleep deeply.

The lesson continued as I became an inquisitive tourist, visiting ancient cities, and learning about the culture. On rest days, for example, I'd join a few others interested in Buddhism for a hike up to Tengboche Monastery to take part in the services there. We'd sit in the back of the great hall, with its huge floor-to-ceiling Buddha, and hang with the monks as they sat on their little square wooden seats, wrapped in thick maroon robes against the chill of the unheated room, steam rising from their bodies as they chanted their ancient prayers. I learned and experienced so much and we had not even reached Base Camp yet. I was determined to drink in every aspect of those seventy days — good or bad.

"The sigh he makes is deep, a hungry air-take for the strength and perseverance all life....takes."
— **Toni Morrison**

Chapter Four
The Faintest Glimmer Is All You Need

"We also rejoice in our sufferings, because suffering produces perseverance; perseverance character; and character, hope.

And hope does not disappoint us."

— Bible

My home is at the end of a mile-long dirt driveway deep in the forest of Saunderstown, Rhode Island. I live near a stream that, in a fifteen minute kayak trip, brings me to the childhood home of Gilbert Stuart, the eighteenth century artist who painted the portrait of George Washington that graces our dollar bill.

I have several other "homes" as well: North Conway, New Hampshire is my home; Talkeetna, Alaska is another of my homes; Yosemite National Park and Santa Cruz, both in California are homes; Davenport, Iowa; Mendoza, Argentina; Jackson, Wyoming; Sedona, Arizona. I could go on and on. I could get dropped off from a helicopter in any of those towns and be a happy home-boy.

Everest Base Camp, at 17,300 feet, is also one of my homes. It is the same elevation as the highest camp on Denali, North America's highest peak at 20,320 feet. For most of the year it sustains no life whatsoever and I knew the longer I lingered, the more I was dying: my body and mind withering at the same slow inexorable pace. It is a place that can rip your soul out a little shred at a time. It is a place of incomparable beauty, monumental views, and devastating fear and anxiety, a place where powerful spirituality coexists with the filth of melted-out privies, a place where childhood dreams subsist together with illness and threat of death.

It was my home for five months over a two-year period as I risked everything to chase my dream.

The most enjoyable day in Base Camp was by far the very first. Phinjo excitedly grabbed my pack and led me over the undulating broken rock and ice to my tent on a raised hump at the northwest corner of our camp. No tents obstructed my view all the way to Pumori behind me to the south, and to the icefall in front of me to the north. My closest neighbors to the west were Scott, the former NASA astronaut, and

51

his climbing bud Adam. In front of, and downhill from my perch was Ryan Campbell's guided group of Rohan and Serge. A bit to my right and slightly downhill were Chip and Vance. From the "front door" of my tent I had an amazing, unobstructed view of the fascinatingly beautiful but deadly Khumbu Ice Fall. My tent was situated so that the icefall and the West Shoulder of Everest loomed large as I entered or exited my crib.

Last year I had a battered old Eureka! tent with a broken fly that allowed the wind to get through the cracks, making many nights a living hell even when tucked into my Marmot forty below zero down sleeping bag. I was thrilled when Phinjo showed me a brand-new three-person brown Eureka! with multiple vents, huge storage space and zippers that actually worked! I thanked Phinjo profusely for his backbreaking landscaping around my prime, hill top real estate. I marveled at my waterfront property which featured a twenty by twenty skating pond of frozen ice a foot thick. Weeks later, as I arrived back to Base from my second acclimatization cycle, the constantly shifting glacier had opened a crevasse about eight inches wide and three feet deep directly in front of my tent. When the sun came out the pond melted down the crack in twenty minutes.

Inside the tent I was in my glory as I unloaded my three duffels of gear and organized the mess. Clothes, hats, glove combinations to the left rear; left front was reserved for my collection of climbing gear, sunglasses, goggles and water bottles; to the right rear was the book collection, pee bottles and electronics; the right front was stacked to the ceiling with boxes of crackers, protein bars, peanut butter and Nutella.

The tent was equipped with multiple storage netting above my head and to the sides, and there I carefully placed first aid supplies, journals, hard candy collection and iPod. The master bedroom suite consisted of two layers of thick sleeping pads separating my puffy Marmot sleeping bag from the frozen foundation, prominently placed in the tent center. Life just wasn't complete until I hung my pictures of Rose and Kurt near the front entrance.

On top of the tent I had two portable solar rechargers, one which would stay at Base affixed by cord, and a lighter get-up that was foldable and would go up the mountain with me. The cords and adapters threaded into openings in the door so that I could recharge in relative luxury. Being a bone guy, my teammates obliged by collecting myriad yak bones laying around camp and these I festooned liberally around and about my tent making my outdoor landscaping décor to die for. I reckoned almost any Everest aspiring chiropractor would dig my pimped crib. It was the bomb, if I did say so myself.

The Puja ceremony was to begin shortly, so I headed over to the six foot cube of stone which had been constructed by a hired stone mason from a distant valley. I recognized the wizened lama from last year as I nabbed a second-row spot on the blue tarp to sit and wait. The elaborate ritual of juniper boughs, incense, multiple Buddhist religious objects and rice for throwing was interspersed with mass quantities of food and drink ranging from tsampa, a barley snack the consistency of butter, to chang, a warm opaque beer with chunks in it. Chips, soda and a lone bottle of whiskey completed the display of offerings. The tsampa was tasty, but after last year I swore off chang and stuck to milk tea.

Our remaining climbers and trekkers filtered in and were joined by guests including Dr. Luanne Freer, the much loved founder of the Base Camp Emergency Room. Our Sherpas looked great in matching caps and OR brand red climbing coats. Phinjo was a former child monk until the Tengboche monastery burned to the ground, and that earned him his position once again to the immediate right of the head lama and Mingma, Crazy Joe's Sherpa, was to Phinjo's right.

Although we "mikaroos" didn't understand a word of the two-hour ceremony, we got caught up in the moment while gazing over the stone stupa to the icefall as the incense and juniper smoke wafted through the air. At one point about an hour into the ritual, a few guys including Danuru, one of the studliest of Sherp climbers, climbed up the stone cube and was handed a twelve foot cedar pole with seven strands of prayer flags attached. As much hooting and hollering commenced, Danuru, expertly placed the butt end of the pole into the cube's center and the masses of flags were unfurled to about fifty yards in all directions and attached sturdily to rocks. On cue, the barley flour was passed around and we smeared it into each others' smiling faces to signify long life and friendship. Our previously placed ice axes, helmets, crampons and harnesses will stay out the night leaning on the stupa for additional safety blessing. Phinjo presented me with a red string suundi previously blessed by the lama. I felt that I had my Karma ... covered.

The Puja was very important to the Sherpas and marked an auspicious start to a safe and successful expedition. To begin climbing into the icefall without the positive blessings and ceremony would be unthinkable. For me, a guy who practices no traditional religion, it struck a spiritual chord, a chance to give thanks for all the people that had helped me to get there to follow my dreams, and to meditate on a safe climb for myself, my teammates and others on "the hill" as well.

When you do the math, there is a hellacious of amount of time spent at Base Camp during an Everest climb. In fact, the vast majority of time at Everest was spent being a slug, because that was the numuro-uno thing on the agenda at Base. The climbing was quite burley, don't get me wrong, but when it's time for R&R after a rotation, sloth and gluttony prevail, and here they were not considered deadly sins.

Here is the skinny on what our (typical) Everest acclimatization plan looked like once we trekked to Base Camp. First, the aforementioned sloth and gluttony for several days, followed by a little shakedown ice climbing on an immense serac (large ice formation that is often unstable and broken off from a glacier) close to home just to check gear. This also gives the Sherpas a chance to roughly evaluate whether the westerner has any clue at all regarding climbing or whether, he or she just bribed someone for a permit. Better to know than not know before the yak-patty hits the fan in the icefall. After this two hour exhibition there will be at least another day of sloth and gluttony (S&G). We ascend the icefall for the first time for two or three hours to about 18,500 feet and stop at the icy feature known as the "popcorn." The jumbled ice blocks, to some, resemble gargantuan popcorn and as the ice blocks are famously unstable, it's a good place to turn around for home. This gives the mildly acclimatized climber a chance to get his boots on the hill, cross a few ladders, do some heavy breathing, and get another grand of elevation for the body to acclimatize to. A return to base and another day or two of S&G follows.

Later, we take a break from ice and go rock, meaning we go behind camp and hike up to Pumori Camp One at 19,000 feet and hang out for an hour lunch where it's safe to laze without threat of avalanche, however the risk of being pooped on by a Gorak (raven) is high on this leg of the journey. You guessed it, two more days of S&G.

Then, however, the climbing gets very serious, very quickly. It was time to go to Camp One above the icefall at 20,000 feet, spend the night, followed by a day hike to Camp Two at 21,500 feet, a return to sleep another night at Camp One before finally heading back to Base Camp. Climbing now was very hard work, a pain festival. The good news was that you had earned two to four more days of S&G.

OK, now it's time for the second big-time acclimatization rotation: up the icefall to sleep at Camp One, the next day move lock, stock and ice axe to Camp Two, hunker down at this higher elevation for three to four nights. It can't really be called S&G here because it is a full-time job just to exist and have a pulse. All of us are deteriorating rapidly at this altitude, but we needed time there for the body to produce red blood cells to carry life giving oxygen to our seventy trillion cells. In other words, we needed to go through this ordeal in order to make a serious bid for all the summit marbles come May. In normal Everest-climbing circumstances we would have taken a little jaunt to the base of the Lhotse Face at 22,000 feet to acclimatize and get acquainted with the route. We were shut down in this regard in 2008 due to the presence of armed climber/guards on the Chinese payroll who made sure no one climbed above that point until the Olympic torch bearers on the Northeast Ridge route in Tibet got to the top or died trying. That's another story. Finally, an early exit after breakfast, and a three-hour dash down the terrifyingly beautiful icefall to Base, lunch, followed by a well-deserved four to five days of S&G.

We turned the "danger dial" way up for the last (before the summit attempt) acclimatization cycle to Camp Three, a veritable pain party at 24,500 feet. First the prerequisite icefall, Camp One, Camp Two for a couple of days, then the ascent up the nearly vertical bulletproof ice Lhotse Face to Camp Three for what most agree is the most miserable night of their lives, then back to Camp Two and finally the dash to home-sweet-home Base Camp. Next, waiting begins for a weather window and the chance, just a chance mind you, of making a summit attempt.

That wait, the break from the completion the last rotation, could range from two days to three weeks depending on the wind and weather conditions. If, however, we have to wait longer than ten days, we can lose precious acclimatization.

That was our plan, but there were multiple variations and any plan had to be flexible to account for the inevitable flies in the ointment. The "Chinese situation" of 2008, the unforeseen months-long fly/ointment combination, affected all our decision-making, always with the threat of not being allowed to even attempt the summit at all. For the brethren (and sistren) of Base Camp the Chinese situation became the topic of endless speculation and gossip.

A little history refresher might be relevant here. China violently invaded the peaceful but backward country of Tibet in 1950. The spiritual head of Buddhism, His Excellency The Fourteenth Dalai Lama, escaped over the mountain passes to exile in Dharamsala, India, where he remains. The invasion resulted in China's claiming half of Mt. Everest. (Should you ever have the extraordinarily good fortune to stand on the summit you will have one foot in Tibet and one in Nepal.) Remember Simonson's demand that each of us sign that document? China has him and any other guide or climber at its mercy because of the reasons I cited in the last chapter. The Chinese will carry the Olympic flame to the summit on the North side — with no one else on the mountain, north or south because China wants no one (read Tibetans who were beginning to demonstrate) to get any publicity that would reflect poorly on the Chinese human rights agenda (or lack thereof). Thus we all had to agree to be no higher than Camp Two until after the Chinese summit with the "symbol of Olympic ideals" (flame). And, of course, we all had to agree not to shoot video or use satellite technology. In fact, this equipment was not allowed in our possession.

All these restrictions resulted in the travesty of having armed guards with shoot-to-kill orders as high as 21,500 feet and the shutdown of communications and Internet use, preventing any potentially embarrassing stuff getting on the web to the world. China reportedly summitted on May 8, though I never saw or heard of the event on any Olympic coverage. We were finally allowed free reign of the mountain so late in the season that our acclimatization could well have been compromised.

In the long run, China hoodwinked us all, including the Nepalese whom they used as pawns to do their bidding. It was fascinating to have two former Soviet satellite inhabitants, Chip from Romania and Jaroslaw from Poland, on the team, to regale us with stories of the similarities between life at Base Camp and their childhoods under Communist rule. Chip told us of his forced military days and one tactic his superiors used to motivate the young conscripts, they declared that when the American imperialists "were soon conquered" then "every Romanian soldier would get a VCR."

An average day for me at Base on a S&G day was to get up around six a.m., pull on my toasty-warm Mammut parka, gloves, hat and hiking boots and gather my empty water bottles and head to the dining tent while trying not to forget glacier glasses and sunblock. The world at this time of day was frozen solid, but by eight a.m. as I finished my fifth or sixth mocha and a two or three-course breakfast, the sun just started to peek over Nuptse, the 26,000 foot giant (nearly the fifteenth 8000 meter mountain in the world) next to our encampment, and the temperature skyrocketed fifty degrees in ten minutes time.

Along with Dean and Crazy Joe, I was typically the first up in the morning, sitting outside while bundled up tightly in the crisp, thin air gazing at the icefall. In the spotting scope, we watched other climbers ascend the bigger ice cliffs on their different schedules. After a group breakfast, several of us would, again, pull chairs from the dining tent and sun ourselves for several minutes before becoming intolerably hot.

The only semi-comfortable place to escape the oppressive heat was the sanctity of my tent. So it's back to the mansion for R&R from the rigors of the morning. I felt compelled to attend to the most pressing matters of importance first off on these mornings so I put on the iPod and spun the dial till I had the rap song "Bust A Move" by Young MC. My goal was, by the end of the trip, to decipher and document Young's poetic lyrics. A sample of his genius is as follows: "Next day's function, high-class luncheon, food is served and you're stone cold munchin'; music comes on and people start to dance, but you ate so much you nearly split your pants". I challenge the most macho of heavyweight champion mixed martial arts cage fighters to read that line and not become just a little moist. My hope was that someday when son Kurt is married, I will stroll to the front of the reception hall, take the mike, and beautifully croon the heartfelt raw emotion of Mr.MC's life work: "OK smartie, go to a party, girls are dancin' and showin' body, chick walks by and you wish you could sex her, but you're standing on the wall like you was poindexter."

As important as this noble quest was, I had other demands on my time, and that was, of course, to construct Shakespearean insults. I am sure Mallory and Sir Edmund himself would have shed tears of inspired awe at my results, if I doth say so myself. Here are just a few of the many I honed to perfection. "Thou bawdy bat-fowling barnacle. Thou cockered clapper-clawed canker-blossom. Thou froward fat-kidneyed flax-wench. Thou puking knotty-pated malt-worm." Take that!

Dispatch: April 10, 2008 Mo-Mo's

Dahl-bat, mo-mo's and Spam all yummy! The first is a Nepali sauce of different vegetables and melted cheese over rice (we have this a lot). Mo-mos, in addition to being a fun word to say, are thin pasta tidbits covering either meat or vegetable or both. Spam is just Spam (spare parts and meat?) I try to eat everything in sight as I tend to lose more weight on climbs than most. On a hard day we can easily burn six thousand to eight thousand calories, so I chow three huge meals plus two to three snacks per day. Six thousand eggs have been part of the six hundred and fifty yak loads that our expedition has required. Tomorrow we walk two hours down trail to Gorak-Shep to treat Phinjo and Passang to lunch. We will be ready for the heavy climbing the day after as we ascend the icefall to Camp One, spend the night, then go to Camp Two then back to Base Camp. A favorite quote from a favorite movie: Anthony Hopkins in "The Edge": *"What one man can do, another can do."* — Dr. Tim out.

End of dispatch.

Most meals also included a variety of Khumbu Valley-grown spinach that I was leery of, having observed many of the tilled fields within inches, in some cases, to the family outhouse. Mid-afternoon meant a snack of Cheese Nips or Wheat Thins and a protein shake.

After several days at Base Camp a mystery had arisen about certain stains high on the walls of the potty tents. It seems that poop was literally flying or the person doing the defecating was standing on his/her head, or both. The only viable explanation was that somehow diarrhea-prone acrobats from the Himalayan Cirque de Soleil let fly while on some complicated maneuver. I hate to be graphic but the stains were five feet up the tent canvas. Maybe the offending depositor was attempting to clean up after himself but it sure didn't seem so.

The nasty nature of the crime was fodder for deep discussion at dinner time. As with the aged population, our bodily functions were fair game for casual conversation. I knew it wasn't me so I could assume a "holier-than-thou" attitude as the investigations continued into the perp's identity.

My theory was that the dreaded HAFE was partially to blame for the crime. HAFE (high altitude flatus expectus) is a documented condition and its one symptom is that you pass gas more at high altitude. (Its physics 101: any gas expands at higher altitude.) I have also observed that some climbers can maintain a constant, almost musical, tone much longer when afflicted, but that was just theory and many more clinical trials must be published to prove that hypothesis.

At 14,000 feet on Africa's Mt. Kilimanjaro in 1999, I heard what I believe was world record gaseous emission length. I am talking minimums of twenty to fifty seconds of same-tone, same decibel scientific samples of toots. I believe that neither Craig John nor Scott Schnackenberg has ever received his rightful place in the record books but I, for one, am damned glad to know them. HAFE has my vote for all-time funniest disease.

There was high anxiety in our community, however, because the perp, (as well as his bowels), was still on the loose. Back to my point regarding HAFE, I posited that since there was higher colonic internal pressure behind the "contents," a sense of extreme urgency in the act of elimination resulted, and the offender prematurely (and before being in perfect alignment to the can) consummated the deed. I left it for other researchers to address why the person didn't clean up. The mystery got so heated that a meeting was called by fearless leader Mark Tucker to address the rising hysteria.

Ironically, just hours before the meeting, I slammed a couple of protein shakes as part of my fifth meal of the day and felt a little uneasy while waiting for the after-dinner gathering. A feeling of bloat came over me as I finished meal number six. I started to sweat as dessert ended and Tuck began the solemn proceedings and at one point I was so full of gas I felt I could levitate. I resembled a sweating, stinking, helium-infused balloon of a climber.

I couldn't pay attention to what Tuck was saying because I was contemplating my escape to the nearest latrine. I finally could stand it no longer and squeezed my way out of the crowded tent with mincing steps, hoping no one would notice. My buttocks were locked so tight I could have opened a Corona with them. With glutes-a-trembling, I tiptoed out the tent door and affixed my headlamp to begin the forty yard obstacle course that led to my relief.

I was in a zen-like trance as I made my way. I was "one with the bum." My focus was intense. I was going to make it! Finally, my objective was within my beam of light. *Where is the freakin' door of this thing*, I muttered with increasing alarm. *damn, damn, damn*. I began to lose hope as precious seconds ticked away. There were only four choices of door for the four-feet-wide tent but I'll be damned if I could find the Velcro opening. I realized that the universe was conspiring against me and all was nearly lost, (in more ways than one, I may add), when with a last-ditch super-human frantic pull, the way was revealed. No time to lose!

"Somewhere children are singing, somewhere flowers grow, but there is no joy for me at all, because, I just soiled myself and the tent wall."

(With apologies to Ernest Lawrence Thayer)

What are the odds of that, I marveled, retracing my steps. *Just as Tuck gives the lecture, I have to illustrate the point.* Shamefaced, I asked Donchere for a pot of boiling water and I stumbled back to the scene of the crime to scrub the evidence. Later, as I looked at the label on the protein powder, I noticed that it touted "New, eight grams more fiber per serving!" I donated the remaining contents to the communal food storage bin.

Typically after dinner people play cards or chess, but not me. I prided myself in knowing not a single card game. The nuances and rules of Go Fish, do not exist for me. My fellow climbers would dutifully ask me to join them, as I filled my empty water bottles with hot water and steeled myself to face the frigid walk back to the tent, but they knew my inevitable response: *It's so sad Vance, that you are so ill at ease in your own head that you must resort to ritual mind deteriorating activities such as whatever game you are playing, just to escape the total misery that is the sum of your mental existence.* As the reader has undoubtedly correctly inferred, I am so life of the party.

New for 2008 was a laptop complete with hard-drive that didn't freeze at altitude and allowed us the luxury of movie nights. Monty or Val would set up the speakers in the storage tent. We would pass around snacks and regale the mesmerized Sherpas with such western cultural movie masterpieces as "Superbad" and "Kill Bill." Pemba was absolutely gobsmacked at Russell Crowe in "Gladiator."

Watching the movies we were clad in our warmest articles but still could not stay warm, especially our feet. We set up elaborate layers of insulation from boxes of supplies to prevent any contact of our boots to the glacier floor, all to no avail. I resorted to my stash of chemical foot warmers but many times I had to leave the storage tent early and hop in my sleeping bag with hot water bottles, just to get the feeling back in my tootsies. Not the ever-smiling Jamling Bhote, however. He never wore a hat or a down coat for movie night and when leaving we marveled at his choice of footwear, rubber Crocs sans socks.

Most days and nights at Base Camp and at the high camps, I would spend hours reading, journaling, studying my notes on sports psychology and reviewing my affirmations and visualizations. Picture me wrapped up in my sleeping bag at Camp Two. The wind is howling outside my tent, the noise so loud I can't sleep. I get out my affirmations, sayings I had copied from many different sources, quotes that really helped me. I snap on my light, hold the paper in gloved hands and recite to myself in a firm, commanding voice: "I love this! I love the grinding, the pushing, the searching, the cold, the danger, the loneliness! It all serves me and makes me stronger and better! And then, "I am totally prepared and have worked extremely hard to be here and I deserve to be here. I honor the mountain by being as prepared as I am." Next, "I will put myself on the line and I will never give up! I will not turn against myself in tough times because I am strong as a yak physically and mentally tough as nails! As long as life exists, there is hope to rebuild, repair, to become more, to emerge victorious in this, my greatest mental and physical battle." I would skip down, find one that is significant for the moment as I lay in the cold grasp of wind that feels like a mighty hand, hell-bent on sweeping us all off this desolate place, a place where humans are just not supposed to be, where sometimes I wondered why I put myself there. "I will take calculated risks and be in the present and let go of the past. I will breathe deeply when tense or scared and have fun and enjoy the journey. I trust myself and will participate one hundred percent without fear of failure." The voice, the words, the wind, the cold, all conjoined themselves together for me. "I am relaxed, focused, and alert. I am alive, alert, well, and enthusiastic. I am a powerful athlete. I am incredibly attentive, talented, and confident. I am in control. I am calm and cool under pressure and I always make the right decisions. I am a masterful, efficient, glorious summit climber of Everest." By the time I finished I was somehow warmer.

"Don't hope – decide."

— Tsering Dokkar Sherpa

One of main things I did differently in 2008 was to make my mind an asset rather than a liability. I read many books that I found meaningful and relevant especially Michael Johnson's book *Chasing The Dragon*. I took notes and reviewed them constantly from my journal. I had brought my copy of *The Secret* by Rhonda Byrne to make sure I was on the beam with the law of attraction.

I simply could not afford to have any negativity or "mind worms" invade my cocoon of focus. Like Big Al Hancock said, "I was here to do a job, simply go to work". And that's what I did — went to work. Many days I spent hours and hours in study and visualization. My mantra was "summit and safe return." In my mind's eye I saw myself, again and again, climbing this great mountain in good style with energy to spare while descending safely through the icefall and returning to Base Camp with all my fingers, toes and a pulse.

A million things can go wrong climbing the "Big E", and, as you will see, an inexplicable series of events occurred that severely tested my will and, in fact, nearly caused me to give up and go home. I very nearly became a quitter: a beaten man for a second and last time at the hands of the world's tallest mountain without even making a true summit attempt.

The last rotation began innocuously enough. I was strong through the icefall, even catching up to people I deemed stronger than me. I was on pace to get to Camp One in personal record time of three and a half hours or less until we got to the jury-rigged ladder section where four shaky lengths were lashed together with rope. The whole assembly was slanted down to the climbers' right and the rickety thing was bridging the gaping maw of a sixty-foot-deep crevasse. It was slow going here and a bottleneck of climbers began to build.

The sun wasn't up so it was bone chilling cold. We stomped our feet and clapped our gloved hands together to get the circulation going as we waited in the growing queue. I passed a struggling Adam who was suffering mightily with freezing hands. I quickly pulled out chemical hand warmers and set to work with Ang Nymga Sherpa kneading some blood flow into his upper extremities.

Finally, it was our turn for the ladder section and we traversed the scary apparatus and picked up the pace to get to camp before the blast furnace of heat came with the sunrise. In our acclimatization travels, we crossed several hundred aluminum ladder sections that were painstakingly installed and maintained daily by the "icefall doctors." The danger these entrepreneurial Sherpas subject themselves to makes Alaskan king crab fisherman look like crossing guards. No wonder some are raging alcoholics. Both years I had set up a ladder in my yard at home and practiced walking with boots and crampons. I felt very comfortable putting my crampon front points onto a rung and dropping my heel down behind, even on these ladders which appeared to be cheap, inferior flimsy. The secret for me was to concentrate on foot placements and resist the temptation to look between my boots to the bottomless depths of the deadly crevasse below me.

Despite our best intentions of an early start, twenty minutes later we got crushed head-on by the sunrise and I wilted under its power as we limped up and down the last few crevasses and stumbled into camp. Nothing subtle about the sunrise on Sagermatha, it's literally a slap of searing heat across the face.

There must have been twenty of us all together at Camp One, just chillin' and hydrating and munching on snacks. I was telling a story of passing the Nepal Women's Team in the first hour of the climb and was shocked at how great they smelled, kind of exotically spiced perfume, or maybe they were just cleaner than me and the people I chose to be with. After all, I took a shower once per month on Everest, whether I needed it or not.

As I told the story, I became alarmed because the Sherpas were just beside themselves with laughter. Big tears were rolling down their cheeks and they spoke excitedly in Nepali. I was concerned I had crossed the line culturally, even though I meant nothing. I usually don't cause international incidents at high altitude (except that one time on Kilimanjaro when my feet smelled like air squeezed from a beached sea mammal) but I wasn't so sure this time. Eventually, it blew over, and I never did get the joke.

The next day we got an early start and went to Camp Two at 21,500 feet, aka Advanced Base Camp (ABC) because it was safely plopped on the moraine out of avalanche danger and we could have dining and cook tents installed by the ever helpful Sherpas. I felt fine on that leg, not super-strong perhaps, but gradually began to lose that sense of strength as we climbed up the last few hundred meters to ABC. I was "popped" but not "knackered" when we pulled over the last huge pile of glacial detritus and our yellow tent town. I was a little concerned that the next time up for summit rotation we would be going from Base Camp directly to ABC without spending a night to rest. I quickly put these concerns on the back burner and chalked it up to a bad day, the first one on the trip. I was due. The next day was a rest day so a "no worries" day and the day after that was to be an easy tromp to the base of the Lhotse Face, a gently rolling ascent of two hours and a gain of a paltry 500 feet elevation.

In the morning, I was wasted. Exhausted. Gas tank on Empty. I was shocked beyond words. We strapped on crampons and with an ice axe in one hand and a trekking pole in the other, set off on this most easy of climbs (relatively speaking of course, because anything at 21,500 feet is astoundingly hard). But from the get-go I just couldn't get my breath and was so fatigued I could barely function. *What the frig is the matter with me?* (Note: I did not use the word "frig"). I had meticulously watched my nutrition but slammed an energy gel anyway just in case, but it did nothing to alter the growing fatigue and frustration. *What's happening to me?* I took two steps on nearly flat terrain and had to stop and rest for thirty seconds just to take two more seriously labored steps while sucking air like a locomotive. *What the flug is the matter with me?* (Note: I did not use the word "flug").

Phinjo, to his credit, said nothing but must have been seriously concerned. A two hour easy hike had turned into more than three hours of physical and mental torture. Had I crossed that line and peaked too early? Could I rebound, and get my strength back before the weather window opened? I was supposed to do the super-serious climb to spend a night at Camp Three the next day. Could I?

I couldn't and didn't as the next day I bagged the climb and opted for more rest at Camp Two and maybe a walk about camp. I didn't have strength even for that abbreviated schedule so I just lazed and stressed about it for two days. Several long, cold nights were consumed by my endless mental loop of questions. What could have caused the flipping of some physiological switch that turned me into such a sorry sack of exhausted protoplasm? To add insult to injury, my stomach started to pain me mysteriously and severely. Sometimes it felt digestive in nature and other times it felt like a severely spasmed internal deep core muscle that I couldn't quite identify.

Days and nights I made small talk with my fellow climbers, but inside I was tortured. No one could help me. I had to deal with it as best I could by myself. My strength had been superb for nearly six weeks. Why had I collapsed nearly overnight? I obsessed day and night at Camp Two while each day planning to try the hike again just to check my status, but I couldn't bring myself to get out there.

I finally resigned myself to having that labored trip to the base of the Lhotse Face be my highest point achieved before making my summit attempt. The date was May 12, 2008, and I was one dejected climber as I packed up and met Phinjo at the dining tent next to the oxygen cache at six a.m. and headed back home to Base.

Little did I know as I began the descent through the valley of silence Western Cwm that my travails were only just beginning. I would have to find the fortitude to fight and win a huge unexpected battle — all this before the expected week-long war known as the summit rotation was to have begun.

Once in Base Camp, I gingerly made my way to the Himalayan Rescue Association (aka Base Camp ER), where the volunteer docs who man the white Quonset-hut tent are funded by each of the climbing groups and by donations. I was checked over but they could think of no reason for my stomach pains. They checked my pulse-oximeter and at ninety percent it was better than most climbers at that altitude (though a reading of ninety percent at sea level would land you in the hospital and under serious scrutiny). Breathing tests came out fine as well. And despite the horrid belly pain, my appetite was still strong. Good thing. Even with a strong appetite, I would have to force feed myself even more than I had been if I was going to survive my summit attempt. At this point, I estimated I was down seven pounds of muscle and would need every ounce to summit and safely return.

In 2007 I had gone down valley to rest and heal in the thicker air but had not planned to do that for 2008. I remembered picking up the gastro-intestinal bug in Pheriche that put the last nail in the coffin of the summit attempt that year. After the Base Camp Emergency Room visit I decided, once again, to risk gut invasion by the myriad third world microscopic terrorists and head down. Maybe more oxygen concentration in Ang Nuru's Himalayan Hotel at 14,000 feet would be a boon to my flagging energy stores. The climbing weather window was still not there and I felt I could safely take two to three full days and three to four nights down low before trekking back up to base, resting two days and then beginning the biggest physical and mental test of my forty-eight years.

Phinjo and I left the next morning and motored down trail before sharing an orange Fanta at Gorak Shep and heading for Lobuche. We probably talked more on this leg of the trip than in any of the previous two years. Phinjo is the kind of guy for whom small talk just doesn't fly. After you take care of the business at hand, there's simply nothing else to say. Perhaps he was excited to be heading home for a few days and for the opportunity to be with his family in Phortse. This was a small picturesque community of superstar Himalayan climbers and their families, many of whom were on our team, having been recruited over the years by Ang Jangbu, a native of the tiny village.

From the get-go I was in radio contact with Mark Tucker for the latest on weather, conditions and gossip from up high. I overheard Dave Hahn sharing his plans with his client Nicky Messner about leaving later than the crowds which is his modus operandi. My plan as well. "Patience, young padawan learner", said philosopher Yoda.

My shoulders were becoming increasingly angry with me as the pack straps were cutting my circulation to the deltoids and traps. Not even my expert ministrations with pack strap adjustments helped a lick as we descended the rocky trail. Finally we rounded a corner and saw the sleepy town of Pheriche still a good four miles of yak pasture away.

What made the hour's hike more bearable was seeing the first green in weeks, living things like plants and occasionally flowers among the rock and stream and yak patties. The yaks and naks had evidently gotten busy because the valley teemed with baby yaks, all balls of fuzziness and full of spunky play.

I loved it and was excited to be there as I opened the door to Nuru's tea house and he greeted me like a long lost friend. I voraciously inhaled his vegetable picadas and fried mo-mo's and delved into the first of many jugs of lemon tea. It tasted better than the previous year. After Phinjo's lunch of dahl-bat, we said our goodbyes as he shouldered his pack and headed home to Phortse. I napped and ate and chatted with the trekkers who came and went.

As the sun slipped over Taboche Peak and Cholatse, the temperature cooled noticeably and at four p.m. a young Sherpa boy fired up the kettle stove in the common room of the tea house by lighting a mixture of dried yak dung and kerosene. I attacked the extensive book collection at Nuru's the next day. The only trouble was many of the editions were in Russian, Japanese, or Swedish owing to the International nature of the Khumbu. I became engrossed in *The Bourne Identity* and the hours quickly rolled by.

Before dinner on May 16, I radioed Tuck and was flummoxed by his report that the weather window was opening and that I should get back to Base double quick. *What do you mean?* I stammered, *what happened, I thought I had time for several days down here!* He mumbled a response that I didn't catch, but I knew the game up here: things change quickly in late May for Everest climbers and I had no time to waste. I had to turn my sorry butt around and climb back up hill tomorrow, well before I expected to. The Everest weather window waits for no one so I just had sit-down, shut-up and get crackin'.

On the spot I decided that I would leave for Base Camp as early as I could get fueled up with breakfast the next morning. Ang Nuru somehow linked a phone call (the phone looked like the old crank up models) to Phinjo's village of Phortse and got me on the line with him to confer on the timing. For some reason, although we could understand each other face-to-face, communicating over the crackly archaic phone system just wasn't happening. Thankfully, Ang Nuru stepped in and acted as interpreter, resulting in the decision that Phinjo would meet up with me on the trail the next day and that I should leave on my own. I ate voraciously, consumed mass quantities of fluids and filled and emptied my pee bottle several times during that last night. If Jason Bourne could get into tight spots, then, McGyver himself out, then so could I.

The next morning found Pheriche enveloped in low hanging cloud. It was impossible to see the next teahouse fifty feet away, let alone the huge snow and glacier covered peaks that surrounded us. By five thirty a.m. I had packed my gear, including forcing my sleeping bag into the nooks and crannies of my backpack. I was the only one crazy enough to be up and ready to party at that hour. After my caffeine fix and fried eggs and chapatti, I hit the trail. Almost immediately I exited the cloud cover and rock-hopped over streams and strode past lazing yaks chewing their cud. For the first time on this expedition I was alone.

The hike to Base Camp from Pheriche demanded significantly more testosterone (or estrogen) on the ascent for the obvious reason that I had 3500 vertical feet to gain over eight hours of constant effort. In contrast, we took four full days to make this same ascent six weeks previous in our pre-acclimatized days. I figured eight hours of leisurely pace stopping anywhere I wished to rest and recharge would allow me to pull into Base about three p.m. After the four miles of relatively flat yak pastures the climb grew steep in a hurry as I took a hard right up dozens of long switchbacks of loose sand. I did not feel strong at all, although being alone it was impossible to accurately gauge my pace. I was fighting rising panic. *What's happening to me?*, I asked myself for the thousandth time. I fought a recurring thought that suggested that *Everest just might not be in the cards for me.* After all, I reasoned, *there's no shame in turning around on Everest, at least I have my life and my fingers and toes.* This thought was tempered by one that repeated the singular question: *Have I done my best?*

Above Dugla, I passed a trekking team and tried to compare my strength to theirs. I was assuming that I should be twice as fast as these newbie hikers ascending the long brutal hill climb to the land of memorial chortens. I depressed myself even further by barely staying in front of them up the long grind. At this point I firmly decided that at the stone seats for porters on the ridge I would call Mark Tucker and Ang Jangbu on the radio and have them pack up all my gear and send it down to me on a yak. I was convinced that with my feeble strength I had no shot to climb the world's highest peak.

> *"Never give up, for that is just the place*
> *and time that the tide will turn."*
> — Harriet Beecher Stowe

Inexplicably, after gaining the ridge, I didn't even sit down for a rest. I just kept walking, head down and straight ahead. Another thought came to me and gradually took hold in my conscious mind: I would not call Mark and Jangbu and quit the climb. What I would do was keep climbing, as long as a shred of hope remained. With increasing conviction I realized that all I needed was a glimmer of hope like a faint light emitting from under a door, to continue the quest. As long as relative safety allowed, and a tidbit of hope existed, I would keep putting one foot in front of the other in the direction of the summit of the world, and my dreams. I was suddenly soaring, like a Gorak riding a thermal. I had emotionally melted down, but had reformed and was made new. I started to feel a tiny bit stronger.

I barely stopped at all on the hike from Pheriche to Base Camp. I ate snacks and drank lemon tea from my water bottles on the way. I stopped only to adjust pack straps when they painfully crushed off the blood supply to my shoulders, or when I had to nitrogenize the rocks next to the trail. I mumbled "Namaste" (this salutation can be used as a hello or goodbye and roughly translates to 'I honor the godliness within you') to the yak herders, porters and trekkers I encountered. I chugged two Fantas in Gorak Shep and thought for sure that Phinjo would have caught up by then. I cruised into Base Camp in six hours. I never told my teammates of the internal battle that waged in my head on that hike. It turns out that I was indeed hammering the pace, which speaks to why I was such a hurtin' buckaroo. The mystery of the fast trekking group remained however. Phinjo never did catch me.

> *"The bruise on the heart which at first feels incredibly tender*
> *to the slightest touch, eventually turns all the shades of the*
> *rainbow and stops aching."*
> —Erica Jong

Big Al and me again at Base Camp, 2010.

Sick and discouraged two days before summit attempt, 2007.

Hitting the celebratory summit bell the minute Big
Al Hancock summitted, 5/19/07, 5:57am.

Sherpani & baby — Pangboche 2007.

Avalanche at Base Camp.

Climbing the Icefall (with a dopey-looking hat), 2008.

Climber rappelling the upper icefall. (Photo: Justin Merle)

Everest sundown 2007.

A scary ladder section, 2008. (Photo: Justin Merle)

At Camp Two with sunset on Lhotse
Face, 2008. (Photo: Justin Merle)

World's highest Chiropractic Adjustment — 21,500 feet, Camp Two, 2007. Big Al is my patient.

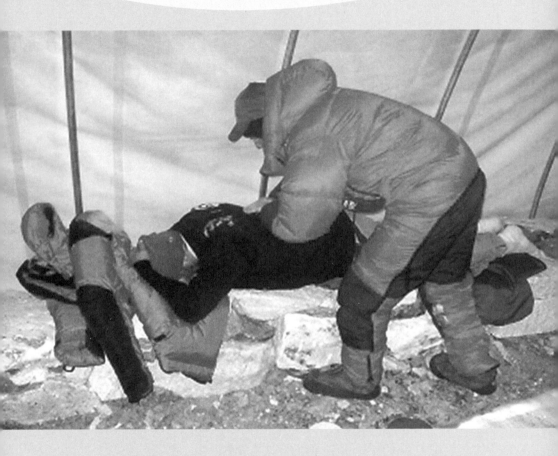

Approaching the Yellow Band — 25,000 feet
[Photo: Val Hovland]

Camp Three foreground, summit pyramid background, 2008. (Photo: Justin Merle)

Curve of the Earth from the summit, 29,035
feet 2008.

Phinjo Sherpa on the summit at 29,035 feet
It was May 24, 2008, 5:11AM.

Luuk Mom... top of the world!

Me kneeling on descent with Walter Laserer
standing 7:30AM 5/24/2008

Hillary Step. (Photo: Nat Smelser)

Looking down the Hillary Step to the South Summit.
(Photo: Val Hovland)

The Khumbu Icefall, end of my dream 2007.

From the South Summit,
looking towards true summit.
(Photo: Justin Merle)

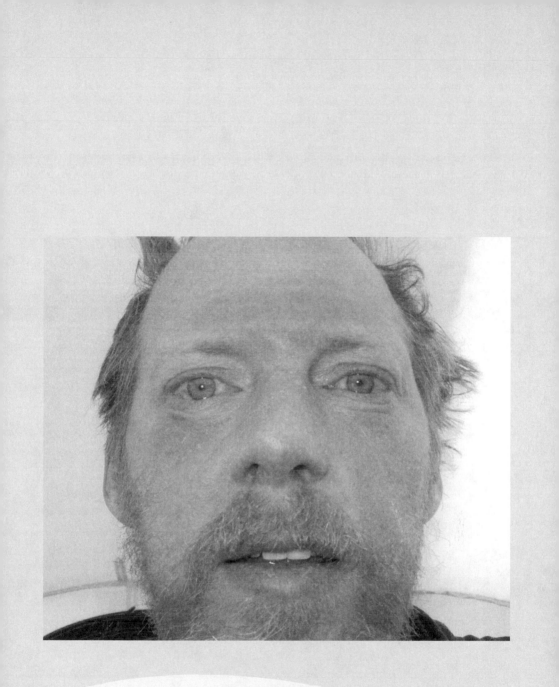

I fell down the ugly tree and hit all the branches,
May 25, 2008, 21,500. feet

With Suchille Sherpa and my son Kurt, May 2010.

CHAPTER FIVE
Thank Your Way To The Top

"It's cold and wet but at least were starving."
— Jimmy Chin

As I made final summit rotation preparations, I was getting mentally pumped as well. I wrote choice affirmations in my mini summit journal which I was taking on the final assault to save weight. I re-read my sports psychology notes for the hundredth time while copying down more key excerpts for the pivotal next six days. I was "getting my shit in one sock." I filed my crampon tips to razor sharp condition, knowing that they would be dulled by the shattered rock layers of the Yellow Band and Geneva Spur. I counted and recounted protein bars, energy gels and hard candies.

I had to do a little laundry so I headed over to the solar shower area with a bar of soap to lather up my lacey underthings (Underarmour underwear and Smartwool mountaineering socks). As I was freezing my fingers in the barely-melted glacial bath water, I was suddenly stunned by an unanticipated feeling. A flash of deep contentment pervaded me as it occurred to me that I had done everything to the best of my ability. I had done everything right! I could do no more to prepare. It was time to do-the-deed. Win or lose, I realized I wouldn't have changed a thing. It was a glorious, deeply calming reverie — a self-hug.

I mentally rehearsed the plan before my meeting with Phinjo: we would once again leave the Puja at four thirty in the morning to be at Crampon Point at five a.m. to spike up and head into the icefall for one last ascent. Reaching Camp One before nine a.m. and the baking sun of the Western Cwm, we would hunker down for about six hours. When the clouds rolled in we'd make a dash to Camp Two, preferably without baking our brains in the blast furnace of the gradual valley ascent between Camps Uno and Dos.

This would be the first time that I would be going from Base Camp to Camp Two in the same day. I was determined not be doing it in blazing sun no matter what, as there was no benefit, especially on summit rotation, in getting scorched. Others in the Everest climbing community saw it differently. In the back of my mind was Dave Hahn's admonition from 2007 that in order to have any chance to climb to the summit you had to have the strength to go from Base to Camp Two same day. I was anxious to test my mettle in this regard.

Once arriving in Camp Two it would be a rest day and the final prep of our high altitude kit. Time to don the one-piece down suit as we would be ensconced in that goose down cocoon for the following three days from Camp Two, to Camp Three, to Camp Four, to summit, to Camp Four, to Camp Two again (we stop only to eat and drink at Camp Three on the way down) — if all goes well that is. Next up would be the climb up to Camp Three at 24,500 feet on the Lhotse Face. This very well could be the crux of the climb as climbers need to pull in to that camp in good stead and without supplementary oxygen.

At Camp Three the summit attempt truly begins. Early in the morning we would don our fighter-pilot designed oxygen masks with eighteen pound tanks, locked and loaded in our packs and head to Camp Four at eight thousand meters or 26,000 feet. At this juncture we will have entered the "Death Zone" where life cannot be sustained for more than a few days even with supplementary oxygen.

After pulling into Camp Four we would hunker down and rest as much as we could under the circumstances. Drinking and eating all we could was crucial to fueling our motors, and hopefully we'd be able to muster a little battery-charging shut-eye.

At some agreed upon time the Super Bowl of climbing would begin anywhere from nine to ten p.m. The idea was to climb to the summit and down to Camp Four before noon the next day to avoid the common afternoon unsettled weather. Of course, summiting is only successful if you return safely, so after a night at Camp Four, post summit, we would descend directly to Camp Two, spend the night, then one last dash across the icefall and back to the safety of Base Camp.

That was the plan and I was sticking to it, even though I knew that on the "Big E" a multitude of things could go wrong at any moment, and quite commonly does. "Adaptability" said Ernest Shackleton when asked to divulge the most important attribute that allowed him and his men to survive in the Antarctic for eighteen months after their ship was crushed to dust in the ice floes. I was learning the lessons of those who had come before me, as I prepared for the biggest mental and physical battle of my life.

"If I have seen further, it is only by standing on the shoulders of giants."
— **Sir Isaac Newton**

Phinjo was all smiles as we met up on this last rest day before summit rotation. He had been following the weather reports and they looked ideal for the pivotal next few days. We needed at least four and preferably seven good weather days to get up and down safely. Our climbing team subscribed to two specialized weather forecasting services for Everest climbers – one in Seattle and one in Switzerland to compare and contrast the data. These forecasts mainly involved two important factors. One was the jet stream winds on the summit, which we want as far away from the summit as possible, preferably The Bay of Bengal, fifteen hundred miles yonder. It was simply impossible to climb in one hundred and fifty mile-per-hour winds. I have turned around on winter Mt. Washington ascents in New Hampshire several times because I literally couldn't stand up in sixty mile-per-hour winds, being buffeted upside the head into submission by the famous "world's worst weather." That 6,288 foot peak has been my mountaineering mecca since my teens.

Factor two was the monsoon season which traditionally nails the high Himalaya starting sometime in late May to early June and makes climbing suicidal due to violent snow fall, high winds and increased avalanche activity. The rest of my team, barring the notable exceptions of Hahn, Sanduk Sherpa and Nicole Messner were already stretched out between Camps One and Camp Four.

It's luck-of-the-draw who ends up on the same schedule as you when you climb unguided as we were. My plan was to wait until the hordes left for the top, those that just couldn't hold their horses after the Chinese delays, including those on my team of IMG. I had observed that Hahn, in 2007 had waited until late in the season when there was less potential delay in critical spots up high. With the route in good shape it made sense to me to bolt for the top on a stomped-in trail with less traffic on the ropes. Ironically, using the same strategy, Dave and group were nearly weathered off their summit attempt at 26,000 feet, as they had to abort one attempt. Fortunately for them, they had enough oxygen to make another bid the next night, and they succeeded.

So the stage was set and I was feeling, all in all, spot-on. I had not let my disastrous last rotation and subsequent painfully weak ascent from "down-valley" put negative "thought-worms" in my head. Now that everything was scratched off the list I needed to hit the fart sack. After dinner at seven p.m. Nepal time 5/19/2008 (a year to the day after my 2007 partner Biggest Al Hancock from Alberta Canada summitted Everest) I crashed.

"I ain't afraid of dyin', I'm afraid of not tryin'."
                                                    — Jay Z

"You don't have to worry about the world ending ... because it's already tomorrow in Nepal."
                                                — Dr. Tim Warren

I was up before I had to be the next morning, eager to get going but with the added attribute of ... fear. It was a combination of loathing for what was to come and excitement to see the project through. I had slept with my climbing pants, high-tech underwear, and fleece on. My gloves and boot liners had been warming in my sleeping bag for the previous hour. The pack was ready I just needed to slip in my ice axe and crampon bag. I pulled on the alveolite inner boots, then the stiff outers and laced both up loosely to avoid shin bruising known as "boot bang." Then I zippered up the built in Gore-Tex gaiters and finally Velcroed the top shut. The whole boot apparatus came nearly to the knees of my six foot frame. I adhered the tent flaps together, said sayonara to my home-away-from-home for the last two months, and set off through the glacial battle zone of rock and ice, and headed for a date with Kaschi the cook.

Although not as friendly as Pemba, the cook from 2007 who decided he could make more money in New Jersey pumping gas, Kaschi was more of a fashionista. He always sported blue jeans, western shirt, fleece and a baseball cap, even on frigid mornings when his first order of business was to light the Buddhist ritual incense. As usual I was the first mikaroo (non-Sherpa) to breakfast and I helped myself to instant coffee, eggs and chapatti. I immediately gagged on each bite and, afraid I would vomit, quickly beat a hasty retreat out the dining tent door. I gradually got my composure but realized there wouldn't be too much in my belly for the four hour marathon to Camp One. I tried some cereal and it was marginally better. I finally slammed an energy gel, filled my two water bottles with hot water and headed outside to check on Phinjo's progress. Having climbed with him for two years, I knew he was no fan of "alpine starts." I pulled on my climbing harness and cinched it down. As soon as it was fastened I feverishly ripped it off and waddled as quickly as possible to the latrine tent. Not pleasant, but at least I was still at Base and not out on the trail.

Beginning again, I slowly concentrated on proper hook-up of my harness as it was a lifeline to relative safety (on all technical climbs). It was a little over-sized on purpose so when worn with the Michelin-man down suit above Camp Two, it would fit perfectly. Finally Phinjo showed up and it looked like it would be the two of us with Mike Hamill and Dasonam Sherpa to push the climb to Camp Two as a make-shift mini-team. We made the two minute hike to the Puja altar and I suddenly realized why Phinjo was a little late, he had already been to the altar and lit the incense and juniper boughs making the oxygen-starved air billow with pungent ritual smoke. Both Sherpas were chanting in their sing-song, nearly under-their-breathe manner. We passed the Puja cube on our right, its cedar pole and prayer flags fluttering their messages to the heavens — and we were off.

During the ten minute tramp to Crampon Point we picked our way around latrines, tents and the occasional yak in the gradually lightening sky. Our metallic accoutrements clanked against each other as we slowly made our way across the undulating wasteland of broken rock and ice mixed with the flotsam and jetsam of dozens of international expeditions and their dream-chasing members.

A forty-foot high serac of blue ice marked Crampon Point and guarded the entry way to the Khumbu Ice Fall, ground-zero for Everest ascents. I pulled out my crampon bag with a feeling of satisfaction at seeing the twenty four newly honed two-inch spikes. After fixing bayonets we slung on the packs and quickly rousted Tuck out of bed with a radio call regarding our departure.

It's critical that I called Tuck periodically. He had to know what time we were leaving any of the climbing checkpoints and what time we arrived. He documented each of our climber's whereabouts and posted them on a poster board. As important to Tuck, was his ability to gauge the strength of the climber in comparison to his companions, a kind of yardstick by which he infers how much gas was in the climber's tank. It's not uncommon for an exhausted climber to hoodwink himself, or the team, with respect to his lack of power.

The slopes were littered with the corpses of climbers who made such mistakes while suffering from the strange disease known as "summit fever."

I have never suffered from such a malady. In fact, whenever I decided that the conditions or my strength weren't up to snuff, I would just turn tail and climb another day. I was even a bit excited about getting another chance at the same mountain. On my first Alaskan Denali expedition, I was in over my head technically and mentally. On that highpoint of North America, the head guide Craig John determined that the threat of avalanche was too high on the 18,000 foot "Autobahn" (so named for all the Germans who had fallen off it, but not to be confused with a different feature on Denali, the "Orient Express," named because, you guessed it, an inordinate number of oriental climbers fell off it). I was thrilled to be able to plan another trip back to tackle Denali again. Rob Scott and I returned four years later and, self-guided, climbed to the top over a four week period in 2004. Same thing with the Grand Teton. It was such a cool mountain environment in Jackson, Wyoming, as well as on the crag itself, that mates Bob D., Scott Schnackenberg and I went back in 2002 to summit "The Grand" after spinning in icy conditions in 2001.

And so there I was, on the biggest, baddest second try in my climbing life and the game was on. That marked my nineteenth trip on the icefall and hopefully my next to last. We cramponed over the smaller ten to twenty foot seracs for forty five minutes before the route steepened. By then we had switched off our headlamps and had to keep moving to stay warm. I had been gagging and coughing since my poor attempt at breakfast earlier, but it let up if I quickly popped a hard candy in the hopper. I had a small five-and-dime store supply of hard candies just for this purpose and one more: it coated the throat and minimized the effect of Khumbu cough. Another lesson learned from the 2007 adventure when I retreated down valley with my throat in a particularly foul mood. I don't normally touch anything with chemical sweeteners, but high altitude was very rough on my teeth enamel and even with judicious flossing and brushing it was a pain-fest in the dentist's chair when I returned home both years.

Anyway, as time went on my gagging became increasingly persistent and obnoxious. Finally, after ninety minutes of spirited, back and forth battle I simply couldn't hold back any longer. In a sudden fit of violent diaphragmatic spasm, I managed to discharge every calorie from breakfast and the energy gels, candies and water I had put in my system since the wee hours. It created an interesting mosaic of sight, smell and texture before it melted its way into the ice. Luckily the four of us were perched on a tilted ten-foot square of broken ice and not on a ladder section. I was on hands and knees heaving my guts out and eventually Phinjo started rubbing my back to comfort me and maybe just to get me to knock it off already. Hamill, putting on his guide hat for the moment, asked me how I was, and I said, *really, I feel great, believe me!* And I did. I was strong, setting the pace for a perfect icefall climb, fast enough to decrease the chance of getting killed by avalanche, yet not so fast as to waste myself.

I was concerned that Mike would suggest I turn-around, or perhaps call Tuck and inform him that I was ill, and that he, in turn, would ask me to spin. In actuality, Mike Hamill, like all guides, was probably keeping his eyes on other climbers even when he was climbing just for himself, and he liked what he saw of me. He knew I was strong, and despite my having blown lunch repeatedly, he kind of inferred that if I was done ruining the view, could we finally get back to climbing. I was worried about my loss of food and water. What little I had been able to force into my stomach was now gone. You simply cannot climb safely at high altitude without fuel in the tank, especially with no water; and most certainly not on Everest. No time to cry over spilled vomitice however, so I quickly inhaled two energy gels, pulled long and hard from my dwindling water supply and aimed my crampon front points to the next snow and blue ice obstacle.

"Be content with what you have; rejoice in the way things are. When you realize there is nothing lacking, the whole world belongs to you."

— Lau Tzu

Maybe it's the cleaning out of my system, and the lightness I felt from the purging. I'm not sure what prompted it, but as I started to move again, an overpowering feeling of gratitude came over me. Maybe this was because I knew I didn't have to turn around like I had the previous year. The thankful thoughts kept rushing through me. I was strong and motivated, and very appreciative. I was so thankful for Rose and Kurt, who loved me even if they didn't totally understand my climbing — and were actually scared to death over it. I was thankful for my wonderful staff who were my biggest fans and supporters and who kept the office going in my long absences while on some exotic climbing trip. I was thankful for all my great friends, climbing and otherwise, who supported me and rooted for me. I was super-thankful to my corporate sponsors and everyday people who dug into their pockets and bought t-shirts or adopted yaks or just purchased dollar stars in the office. I was filled with gratitude for Palmer, my doggie (his shedding white coat had left traces in my equipment bag on Everest). As I climbed each rung of a ladder, the sense of thankfulness kept coming. I felt like one of those Oscar recipients thankful to a long list of people before the orchestra finally drowns him out. I felt connected to all of them in the early morning deep-freeze of the Khumbu Icefall. I felt all of them at once almost pushing me up the ice blocks, and I felt supremely honored to have earned their support. I remembered the ancient Chinese adage that all humanity is connected by an invisible red filament, and at 19,500 feet, I felt the love.

Most of all, I was overjoyed to be living my dream … to be doing it, after dreaming and training for years. I was putting one spiked Frankenstein boot after the other in the direction of my dreams. I was so lucky and I knew it. How many people get to live their dreams and experience such an amazing journey? At that very moment, whether or not I made it to the top of that hill was inconsequential.

I was appreciative of Phinjo's quiet concern. I remembered that he cried right next to me in 2007 when I was so ill in the icefall, and made the tough but appropriate call to quit. I was grateful for each step as the hours crept by. It's hard work climbing the Khumbu icefall, but I had a lightness to me that I had never experienced before and haven't since. I was so happy just to be propelling my body – which reminded me of my vintage four-wheel-drive Land Rover Defender, a superbly tuned, un-stoppable machine.

I was thankful for my parents who early-on gave me a love of travel and living out-of-the-box. I was appreciative of Dr. Matt who was adjusting all my patients. I was grateful to my patients, many of whom supported me monetarily, and all of whom supported spiritually.

"The dude abides."
— Jeff Bridges in 'The Big Lebowski'

Three and a half hours after the spikes went on four of us pulled over the final serac, climbed over the avalanche-prone rock-strewn "football" field, went up and down a couple of monster crevasses and suddenly we came face to face with the tents of Camp One at 20,000 feet, the first way station on our quest for the top of the world. I had never felt even close to this good at Camp One. I really disliked this camp actually. I had a severe altitude induced migraine here in 2007 that felt like a railroad spike had impaled itself in my temple. A condition caused by my failure to drink enough fluids, another lesson learned. The winds at night blew through there like out of control locomotives. It was just so cold there in the mornings that people fumbled around like zombies in slow motion as they tried to get moving in the mornings. Hamill told me that when he was guiding two clients there in 2006, a huge avalanche rampaged through the camp, just decimating the temporary tent town. It was a miracle that there were so few injuries and that no one died, but Tucker to this day is upset that he lost his down suit. If he waits long enough he could probably retrieve it in years to come, as all manner of abandoned or lost objects work their way through gravity and avalanche, eventually ending up in Base Camp. Body parts, helicopters and climbing supplies from decades past share space with the broken ice and snow of the Khumbu Icefall, and inexorably descend, in some form, to Base Camp and below.

The cold and wind was denied by the blast furnace heat of a cloudless, windless day at Camp One. That's our predicament on May 20, ... smokin' hot. But again the plan was to rest until it cooled in the afternoon clouds, hydrate and eat everything in sight. It was especially imperative for me to accomplish these tasks, as I was seriously depleted from a nearly four hour marathon of life threatening ascent while demonstrating the "technicolor yawn." The good news was that since we had the camp to ourselves, we could each stretch out in personal tents for naps. It was so hot in my tent that even with all the vents open and me naked with no body parts touching, it was barely tolerable. Mike sparked the stoves as I gathered snow to melt, and we set about the job of hydrating. We were joined by Walter Laserer, an Austrian mountain guide, and his client, a non English-speaking German.

Despite my disdain for the camp, it was a fascinating and beautiful place. I was able to get some snooze time in before the first clouds moseyed overhead a little earlier than expected at two p.m. Phinjo shyly asked if I was ready to go. *A little more eating and drinking bro,* I replied. The truth was, I wanted more cloud cover. Magically, the clouds closed in just like we had hoped, and we saddled up. I was so tickled to be making this Camp Two jaunt the same day as leaving Base Camp that I was giddy.

I felt great but my enthusiasm was tempered by my history of severe exhaustion on this stretch over the previous two years. This year was worlds better than 2007 when I was so slow that I just totally embarrassed myself in a puddle of pain, literally, taking one step and resting thirty seconds before forcing myself to take another, for hours and hours, a mentally and physically brutal experience.

My two 2008 ascents through the Western Cwm had been significantly better but still painful. Once, when climbing the last lip of glacial moraine to our camp at 21,500 feet, I was so knackered with fatigue that when I was greeted by Nicole and Hahn, I couldn't even respond. I barely got my pack and crampons off before collapsing supine onto the nearest rock resting place.

The route from Camp One to Camp Two began with some gargantuan crevasse crossings, some ladder crossings and hairy proximity to the northwest Nuptse face. There are some terrifying hanging glaciers that most definitely will avalanche soon. I hoped for all our sakes that it would happen in June when the climbing season was long-gone, otherwise alpinists would be squashed into unrecoverable DNA sized portions. This was the rub of climbing Everest: manage risk. Take the route nearest to Nuptse and make better time, but expose yourself to a greater likelihood of deadly avalanches. We took the faster and hairier route, and ascended the gentle undulating terrain after the big crevasses.

I set a good pace for myself by rest-stepping my merry way very slowly. Rest stepping works miraculously for conserving energy but is slow as molasses running uphill – in winter – on Everest.

After an hour and a half we crested a small ridge, moved out to the center of the Cwm and for the first time could see our objective: the first tents on the moraine next to Everest's Southwest Face. I knew from experience that the destination never comes if you obsess about it, so I focused on clipping into the rope, (hidden crevasses abound) and putting one foot in front of the other. I was delighted that the clouds stayed put with only a few breaks of sun. I was dressed perfectly for this schizophrenic environment where you needed to vent your body heat when the sun breaks through, but button up for the overcast skies. The temperature could and would swing fifty degrees almost instantaneously.

Mike and Dasonam got a little ahead of us, but I didn't care, as we were making great progress, finally making it to the lower tents on the moraine. You know I didn't like Camp One for its cold and wind. Camp Two makes me nervous for another reason entirely: hidden crevasses. One of the most famous Sherpas of all time, Babu Chirii, died here several years ago by falling into a crevasse that was covered by a snow bridge. Chirii was famous for his speed ascents of Everest and for once staying on the summit for over twenty one hours without supplementary oxygen.

In 2007 I had seen a hole where a climber's body had penetrated a similar crevasse but had been saved by his outstretched arms on the way down. The hole was black and bottomless as far as I could discern. The Sherpas joke that if you fall in a crevasse on Everest you will pop out in America. The ironic thing is that this dangerous area was only thirty feet from the safety of the glacial moraine of Camp Two. Like the entire Everest climbing experience no one ropes up together. Roping up (tethering two or more climbers together by an outstretched climbing rope) would protect you in a crevasse fall but would add to the risk in places like the icefall and especially the steep Lhotse Face. Here in this spot roping up would be a safe decision, but no one, including ourselves, ever did. So I guess we, like Babu Chirii before us, were rolling the dice.

The usually hellish climb from the relatively flat glacial Western Cwm to the three hundred feet or higher tent site of our Camp Two was easier than ever for me. No counting games of twenty steps then rest in a futile attempt to distract myself from the grinding misery. The terrain was changing rapidly due to the daily melt of spring warmth trumping the nightly deep freeze of the great mountain's west side. Converging streams of melt water gnawed their way through the previously bullet proof ice and rock conglomerate causing us at times to dance, in twelve point crampons, from rock to ice hillock, back to rock all the way up.

Gratitude continued to surge through me as I was so thrilled to be allowed to test my mettle on this, the greatest mountain in the world. The higher I went, the more I felt the climb was my personal canvas, the background of which I had been painting for several years. And there I was rapidly brush stroking a grand finale. My personal masterpiece, my mission, my purpose, my Everest summit attempt. Whatever happened from then on, and a world of things could go wrong, I had done my best and was in the process of doing my best. It was the most glorious feeling in the world.

There was a crew of survivors at Camp Two that evening besides the group that I had come up with that day. We had Ryan Campbell's guided group of Rohan Freeman and Serge Massad, as well as the team of Val Hovland and Monty Smith with their Sherpas Phunuru and Passang Rinjing. Word came at the nightly radio call that our earlier summit team had left Camp Three but two of our brethren, Scott Parazinski and Bob Lowry had turned around from a blown lumbar disc and exhaustion respectively, and would be heading down the next day to join us at Camp Two. Their summit dreams were over. However, we had Vance, Chip, Crazy Joe, Kurt, and Adam from our team who would be getting into summit position the following day at Camp Four. They were just entering the Death Zone.

After dinner I headlamped my way back to the tent and started sifting through gear and getting my head wrapped around the job to come. Almost as soon as I got back to my tent I started to gag once again. Usually all I had to do was get a hard candy in my mouth to calm things down, but this was different. I couldn't stop. I loudly lost my dahl-bat dinner outside the tent. I looked around to see if anyone had witnessed my offerings to the mountain gods and saw a face look out from the tent across from me and immediately look away. *Shit, Shit and double shit*, I muttered under my breath in disgust. My worst fears were realized: Ang Passang had seen me!

Ang Passang was the autocratic climbing sirdar, kind of a vice president in charge of Sherpa climbing activity above Base Camp. At Camp Four he was known to browbeat climbers who were too lethargic in getting out of the tents for their descents. He was just doing his job, of course, but nevertheless I was scared of him. I had gotten the distinct impression in 2007 that he didn't think much of my fitness and climbing attempt. I thought that he may have been upset that his employee Phinjo missed out on a bonus (climbing Sherpas at IMG get their entire fee only if the client reaches Camp Four) even though I had given "The P Man" a generous tip before leaving camp that year.

If he was suspect of my abilities in 2007 I really couldn't blame him because, I did suck. Maybe I was reading too much into it, but unlike the other Sherps, Ang Passang wasn't terrifically friendly in 2008. I just kept my distance. The long and short of it was the sirdar could torpedo your summit attempt if he deemed you unworthy. My stomach contents being expelled in front of his tent at this stage of the game was not going to endear me to him, especially if he suspected AMS or HACE (acute mountain sickness or high altitude cerebral edema). He could radio Ang Jangbu, who could talk to Mark Tucker who could satellite phone conference with Eric Simonson in Seattle who could suggest that I retreat and with the monsoon season closing in, that would be it for me, done forever on Everest just because I colored the snow a different shade. None of those conversations happened to my knowledge. I wasn't sick, just nervous and hyper. I hunkered down in my tent for the evening and listened to the B-52's and

The Offspring, then mellowed out to some Lucinda Williams and John Mayer.

As usual, bright and early, I made my way to the yellow Quonset hut dining tent which was set up for the season on a more or less flat section of gravel and ice. Stones had been set around the perimeter for seating. It was always way below freezing in the early morning and after dinner, so we would pile up extra gear or sleeping mats on the rocks as additional insulation for our bottoms despite at this point living twenty four – seven in our down one piece suits. I started the day the same way as in Base Camp or home in Rhode Island for that matter, coffee. Here at 21,500 feet, four miles straight up in the air from my North Kingstown, Rhode Island home, the coffee tastes just as good, even though it's instant and the water has little, white unidentifiable floaty things in it. In order to get maximum hydration I would refill the hot water when my mug was half empty and only add more coffee every fourth cup. Until it ran out, I would also add hot chocolate mix and just pound back the mixture. *Hydrate or die.*

I hoovered up dry cereal, eggs, bacon and chapatti pancakes as people gradually filtered in from the tents. My job for the last rest day in the expedition was to laze, eat, organize gear and upper mountain food, check, and recheck it all over again. I wiled away the time by reading my journal of affirmations and sports psychology notes.

Later that day poor Scott and Bob came down from Camp Three just all beat up. Scott had a severe back injury flare up on him above 24,500 feet. In severe pain, he was barely able to stumble down the steep ice of the Lhotse Face. Bob Lowry, one of the funnier dudes on the team, had run his gas tank bone dry with his effort to get to Camp Three and had absolutely nothing left. He very wisely turned around. Their physical pain was rivaled only by their mental pain after having failed to meet the objective, the goal, the raison d'etre. I poked my head into Scott's tent to offer my condolences and he said to me, "I have a really great life and I don't need the summit to make me happy." I wasn't sure if he was telling me, or telling himself.

OK, it's going down! Everything was done. All I needed to do was get some sleep because I would, anyway you sliced it, be severely sleep deprived from then on. I awoke at three thirty a.m. on May 22, 2008 and once again stumbled over the broken rock moraine to the dining tent where I was surprised to see another climber. Usually I am the first. It took me a while to identify him, as he was hunched over with his head in his hands and bleeding profusely out of his nose into one of the large metal pots that the Sherpas use for food prep. It was Monty, who in preparing for his summit attempt, told me that his nose, for whatever reason, started to hemorrhage and wouldn't stop. Blood was everywhere. It had soaked through whatever he had found for towels and an alarming amount had collected in the pot. The Sherpas, Monty and his teammate Val were in contact with HRA in Base Camp by radio, but nothing seemed to be working — even the nose tampons that they tried to construct. There was nothing I could do but give him my well wishes. (I later learned that, indeed, the bleeding didn't stop even after retreating to Base Camp, and down valley. He had to be flown out in a helicopter rescue to Kathmandu with a loss of over twenty percent of his blood volume.) His summit dream was over. Mine was still in the works. I harkened back to my success affirmations to keep my climbing focus.

Phinjo and I met outside the tent and nodded at each other, nothing to say now, just to do. Wordlessly, we fixed the crampons to our boots and cinched down our harnesses. There was nothing left to do but go up, way up. Mike Hamill and Dasonam were again in lockstep with us, Rohan and Panuru (not to be confused with Phunuru) joined in. We started up the broken ice ridges of camp and got into the more subtle grade and undulating terrain of the upper Western Cwm. It truly was living up to its moniker as "The Valley of Silence" on this frosty morning.

I was psyched to get a move on and was supremely thankful that my gagging was somewhat under control when Hamill whispered under his breath that we needed to pick up the pace. I was honored that Mike was giving me support along the way and almost imperceptibly we started to move faster. After an hour or so we arrived at the base of the Lhotse Face, the most imposing of sheer walls. When Phinjo and I were here on my falling-down moments of fatigue on the last acclimatization rotation we had seen rocks the size of suitcases tumbling wildly down the face nearly decapitating several climbers affixed to the rope.

Not every climber wears a brain bucket (helmet) on this section but I did, realizing full well that if I took a head shot from anything bigger than a golfball, I was toast, helmet or not, and would likely be the next guy in whose memory a chorten would be constructed at Thokla Pass. Scrawled on my helmet was my blood type "A+". This was a poor attempt at gallows humor because if any of us ever needed a blood transfusion, a supply and a phlebotomist would have to be delivered from home. I did hope that Monty hadn't seen my lid that morning.

Hours rolled by and we made gradual vertical progress. Through much of the climb it seemed that we were in a battle against nature: the weather, the terrain, the lack of oxygen, and Sir Isaac Newton all conspiring against us, but sometimes you found yourself just cruising, and despite those self-same adversaries you somehow wound up on the same team again.

We were in the flow, albeit painfully. We were winning the battle — on points. The outcome of the war was far from being known, ten thousand things could go wrong, still, after all this time, effort and focus. No whining though, because it was a fair fight and the glory was just being able to put one foot in front of the other and make it six inches forward and six inches higher with each labored step and each pull of the jumar on the rope.

Blessedly, the day was partly cloudy with a light wind so I stayed comfortable with the down suit unzipped down to my waist. *So far so good*, I thought to myself as we clipped into a rope anchor with Ryan and Serge to have a drink and a five minute rest before shooting an energy gel into my mouth and continuing up the endless rope. After five hours and twenty minutes, and after passing two dozen tents of other expeditions, we were able to see the yellow Eureka! tents of our Camp Three at 24,500 feet. Our camp was in a small ten foot wide area that had been hacked out of the ice by our illustrious Sherpa team and was held on its perch by a spider web of ropes which were anchored into the flanks of Lhotse by snow stakes and ice screws.

"Climbing is hard, but it's easier than growing up."
— Ed Sklar

I was deeply gratified to be there. I was tired, but definitely not wasted, incredibly better than when I was last there in 2007, and far better even than during my ill-fated journey from Camp Two to the Lhotse Face bottom ten days previous. (I was still unable to rationally ascertain the reasons behind my total exhaustion of the previous acclimatization rotation.) There I was, thousands of feet higher but feeling much better, go figure. It made no sense, but I didn't care a lick because I felt great (except for the continued gagging that is).

I pulled out my British Royal Air Force designed Top-Out oxygen mask and regulator and wrestled one of the eighteen pound bulky IMG oxygen bottles from the back of the tent and plugged in at one liter/minute resting flow. Everyone else on the mountain used Russian Poisk oxygen bottle systems that have no heavy regulators but less capacity. I was waiting for this moment on the climb for a long time. From now on we would be sucking supplementary oxygen and thank God. We were nearly into the Death Zone where, even with oxygen, our bodies and minds would be very slowly disintegrating, dying, even while just sitting. It was estimated that supplementary oxygen lowers the effective altitude by about 3000 feet. In other words, with "gas" we had the physiologic oxygen usage of 21,500 feet while at Camp Three's 24,500 foot actual elevation.

Phinjo came by with hot drinks and a little later with boiling water to cook up our freeze dried meal du jour. I had the tent all to my lonesome and good thing, because I started my obnoxious gagging once again. I just couldn't stop coughing and croaking even with my hard candies, and every two minutes I yelled an apology over the wind to Serge and Ryan, two flimsy tent fabrics away. I must have been driving them nutty. An hour later I leaned over and before I could zipper the tent door completely open, threw up over my bandana, buff, food bag, and plastic dish and cup, half in, and half out of the tent. (Totally nasty clean up while whispering bad things under my breath, but for the remainder of the trip, I never did my weird coughing/gagging combination or vomited again). Could the fact that I was plugged into supplementary oxygen have countered the "nerves" of the summit attempt so far?

Supplementary oxygen has a big time warming effect which I learned first-hand in 2007 at Camp Three. I was freezing my rear end off even with being inside two sleeping bags and down suit that year as I only had one sleeping pad instead of two to insulate my body from the glacial ice. The intent, when there on an acclimatization cycle, was to get used to the thin air, and to use supplementary oxygen only in emergency. After not sleeping and having to sit up to minimize my surface exposure to the tent floor for hour after painful hour while freezing to death in minus twenty degree air, I said *this sucks,* and plugged into oxygen. Almost instantaneously, I passed out in a deep sleep and total warmth. I got off the tank another time that night, and then back on, with the same warming effect and instantaneous sleep. On the summit attempt however, the name of the game was to rest, be warm and stay strong because the summit attempt really began there at Camp Three. I was plugged into "gas" for virtually all of the ensuing seventy two hours.

Over the radio I learned that Rohan had turned around somewhere between Camps One and Two and ended his dream to become the first African-American man, as well as the first Jamaican native to summit. More summit dreams were kaput.

I wrote a little, called in a dispatch to Joe in Rhode Island on the satellite phone, and crashed early after checking and double checking my gear. We would be out and gone by six a.m. so I planned to stir early at 3:30 to prepare. The very first vertical step and each subsequent one would be the highest I had ever been in my life. I was so happy and thankful, again, just to be there and "in the game."

> ### *"Is it dangerous? What is dangerous is*
> ### *not living your dreams."*
> #### — Dr. Tim Warren

The dawn was clear and cold with negligible wind on May 23, just about perfect conditions for the day's long climb to the worlds' highest camp nestled among rocks at the South Col at 26,000 feet, a four to seven hour stint away. The snow gave a perky squeek as each of the twelve crampon points dug deep. I have always loved that sound when the points sink in. You innately know you have great purchase and are connected to the mountain. It's a feeling of being in the right place, at the right time, working with nature, and in the flow.

I have never had the attitude that I was conquering any mountain. I realized that I was nothing more than a bug on her side and could be squashed at any moment. So far I had been "allowed" to climb big mountains, nothing more. I could never fathom the cocky audacity to "conquer" any mountain and especially not Everest, Sagarmatha: Goddess Mother of the World.

We had to traverse about fifty nerve-wracked yards to pick up the fixed lines out of camp. We had to dodge tent lines and all kinds of rope used to strap the tents on the mountain because of the incredibly tenuous space they occupied on the Lhotse Face. I was appreciative that we set the IMG Camp Three much higher on the Lhotse Face than camps of other groups because it was going to be a very long day even without adding another hour of tough ascent to the total.

It was mesmerizing to watch the gossamer bag inside the oxygen re-breather bottle expand and contract in slow motion with each labored inhalation. I felt a calming sense of safety even if there really wasn't any to be had, anywhere. We clipped into the fixed line at six a.m. and started the ascent up the remaining 500 feet of the Lhotse Face. It was Phunuru, Val, Phinjo and me. Mike, Dasonam, Ryan, Serge and Panuru would leave right behind us.

Val had rallied from her later than expected arrival at Camp Three and was busily filming as well as climbing. I was just totally concentrating on the climbing, and my engine and transmission. I had a virtual dashboard in my mind with multiple gauges. *Energy? Hydration? Too hot? Too cold? Should I eat? Should I drink? How was my technique with cramponing? Was it efficient? Do I need to alter or change foot placement to balance the muscle load? Is my rest step correct? Do I need to zip/unzip?*

My right foot started to get cold, very cold. *How could this be,* I queried myself, *It's doing the same thing the left foot is.* With a start I realized that I had made a very amateur blunder. I had not removed my Spinal-Pelvic Stabilizer orthotics from the triple layer boots to dry out in my sleeping bag while I slept. Moisture from the previous day's climb had frozen in my boots and in the below zero temperature was slowly, painfully reminding me of my oversight. Dopey slip-ups like this have cost people body parts.

I constantly curled my toes and wiggled them to keep the circulation going and gradually they re-warmed. It was exhilarating climbing because it was higher than I had ever been. As I leaned into the mountain to rest between kicking steps into the near vertical ice, I could look through my legs to astounding views thousands of feet down. Camp Three was not far away but almost straight down! At times it was so steep that the fixed rope disappeared below me. The steepness of this vertical world combined with the fact that my head was hanging down as I stared at the precipitous view between my legs made me suddenly dizzy. Still, I couldn't tear myself away. The sheer ice all the way to the vast Western Cwm and Camp Two was sandwiched by the massive Nuptse on my right and the west shoulder of Everest on my left. At the end of the Cwm lay Camp One and the beginning of the icefall where it plunged over the abyss. Cloud cover crept nearly up to the highest seracs of the icefall as the early morning progressed. Beyond the clouds obscuring the icefall was the stunningly beautiful Pumori, and beyond that still, Cho Oyu, the world's sixth highest mountain deep in Tibet.

I felt no fear. I was simply astounded at where I was and what I was seeing. I tried to imprint the views in my cerebral cortex because it was far too exposed for me to fumble with my pocket camera on its leash around my neck. For the same reason I would take no more than a handful of pictures over the next two days.

After ninety minutes we traversed the icy Lhotse Face, started heading north, and made for the Yellow Band, a vertical yellowish fifty foot rock layer at about 25,000 feet. A vicious unexpected wind blew down from above, a harbinger of the tougher climbing to come, with the added torment of reduced oxygen availability with each step. We were officially in the "Death Zone."

I clawed my way up the initial vertical thirty feet of the Yellow Band in clumsy style. My ice climbing gloves had become impregnated with ice crystals and banging my gloved hands on my legs did nothing to dislodge the stuff. Thus my grip was dangerously compromised even though I had good bite on the rope with my jumar (the jumar, or ascender, is a metal device clipped to my harness, that once attached to the rope, allowed it to glide through as you ascend, but steel teeth prevent a backward rope movement). My crampon front points clanged uselessly against the featureless rock, denying any lower body purchase on the rock at all. To get over the lip of the rock I did pull-up after pull-up using entirely too much upper body. As I finally clambered over and flopped like a fish out of water at the top, the cold wind bore down relentlessly. I fought dizziness as my respiration rate was off the chart, and I could feel my pulse like jackhammer blows inside my skull. My resting pulse rate while sunning with Rose on Narragansett

Beach would be a laissez-faire fifty beats-per-minute or less. Lying on my heaving gut at the top of the Yellow Band at 25,000 feet on Everest, in near zero temperature with God knows what wind chill, I wouldn't have been surprised if I was blowing two-hundred.

Scrambling off after catching my breath and calming myself, I realized that I wasn't really at risk of dying on the Yellow Band, as the jumar would have held me to the rope. But it was a moment that for the first time, probably since the first attempt on Denali in 2000, I hadn't felt in control. In fact I felt panicked. I hoped against hope that it would be the last of those experiences. I should have guessed it wouldn't be. After all, this was Everest.

The Yellow Band pitch had left me shaken (but not stirred), so as I continued on easier terrain I gathered myself, focusing solely on the business at hand — good crampon placement, quick rest step making sure to rest on the bone structure and not the muscle to save every last microgram of energy, and safe and efficient transfer of the safety carabiner and jumar. I was scanning the dashboard of bodily function and performance gauges constantly, and was quickly in the zone mentally. I decided to not let panic gain even a little edge into my thinking because, no doubt, the Yellow Band presented just the first of many opportunities wherein clear thinking and proper execution must prevail.

A long traverse of a snow slope led to the downward sloping broken shale which began the monstrous stone feature known as the Geneva Spur, the moniker given by the Swiss expedition of 1952. Just before the Spur an exhausted descending climber was stumbling towards us. He stopped for a second next to me and just fell ass-over-tea-kettle. Luckily for him he was still clipped into the fixed line. Otherwise he would have quickly been reduced to a red streak of tissue spread over 3,000 vertical feet. Before I could mentally process this event, Phunuru unclipped and rushed to his aid in blazing speed and at his own peril. In his mentally befuddled state, the climber, in the course of trying to right himself, was attempting to unclip his safety loop. Phunuru screamed at him to stop. He listened and allowed Phunuru to help him to his unsteady feet and on his way.

Phunuru is a principal educator in the Khumbu Climbing School, an organization designed to improve medical training, climbing and mountaineering skills among the Sherpa. Foreign teachers included some of the biggest names in American mountaineering such as the late Alex Lowe, Conrad Anker and author/climber Jon Krakauer.

Although a bit of a non-sequitur, I thought this story humorous. Phunuru, who, like most Sherpa, would have little need for a car or driver's license as there are no roads in the valley, let alone any sort of motorized vehicle, had earlier recounted an account of a trip to Spain at the behest of a mountaineering client of his who was a big-time Barcelona banker. He suggested to Phunuru that it was about time for his first driving lesson. So, in the city's busy downtown he took the wheel ... in the man's Ferrari.

We crossed paths with Kurt Wedberg and Adam Janikowski from our IMG family as they exhaustedly made their descent from their successful summit the day before. The Geneva Spur was mostly broken rock with little snow, so thankfully we removed crampons and kicked steps with our boots as we slowly moved up. Our oxygen setting since starting that morning was on the typical climbing flow of three liters per minute and it felt good. I would not have a prayer of summiting this mountain without supplementary oxygen. Only the freaks of nature, the superstars of climbing could gut thru such a process. The first persons to ascend Everest without supplementary oxygen were Austrian Reinhold Messner and German Peter Habeler in 1978 and some consider this to be the first "true" ascent. People who can climb an 8,000 meter (26,000 feet) mountain without oxygen are like the Lance Armstrongs or Michael Jordans of mountaineering.

Several hours into the climb, we had made slow gradual progress up the Spur when suddenly the terrain eased and a traverse began from south to north. Twenty minutes later tents appeared. I could barely believe that I was at the South Col, the saddle of windswept rock and ice between Lhotse and Everest.

After years of reading about this place, failing to get there the year before, and climbing all morning in the altered state of high altitude, I was just plain disbelieving. It was 11:30 a.m. on May 23, as we were greeted by the inhabitants of this strange village. This was one of the most debilitating and deadly places to be on this earth. People can only survive a few days there even with supplementary oxygen. Two days previous a thirty something Swiss climber had climbed up to this camp and promptly died in his tent less than fifty feet from mine.

IMG Everest Dispatch from Eric Simonson
Dispatch #39 May 23, 2008
IMG leader Ang Jangbu reports that Justin, Dean, and Jaroslaw made it back to the Col about noon (Nepal time). Tim, Val, Hamill, Ryan, and Serge made it up from C3 and are also at the Col now. Adam and Kurt are on their way down to C2. Nicky and Dave are taking

another rest day at C2. Chip, Vance, Joe, and Rohan will be back in BC soon.

End of Dispatch.

Despite the death-inviting conditions, some of our Sherpa friends are actually happy to be at the South Col. All are really strong dudes but aren't, as of yet, "summit Sherpas." They were there at 26,000 feet to cook and melt ice for drinking water and pay their dues in order to, down the road, achieve "summit Sherpa" status. Its worth Camp Four's mind and body numbing environment for some, if it means getting brownie points with Ang Jangbu and Ang Passang.

The Sherpas kept the tents and equipment from blowing away in frequent storms. They also kept the stoves going and ice melting for pre and post summit climbers who were the mental equivalents of slow four-year-olds at that altitude and level of exhaustion.

It was time to hunker down and get organized for the final assault at nine or ten p.m. First order of the day was to replenish fluid levels, then chow down and repeat all day while resting on my backside. Second order of business was drying layers of boots and gloves. I relearned that lesson, painfully, on that morning's ascent with frigid foot.

To my minor horror I realized that my food bag never made it up to Camp Four with the equipment carries. However, Monty's did, and since he was being helicoptered out with excessive blood loss, I pilfered the contents. I was amazed that I didn't have my panties-in-a-bunch with this news. Normally on a summit day, I would have my "Type-A" anxiety going on and every upset would raise my blood pressure another few millimeters of mercury. It was incredible to me that on the biggest mountain in the world, and certainly on my biggest day of danger and uncertainty, I was well-within myself, focused and relaxed.

This is a new experience, I mused. The stress-less mindset deteriorated as I rested and tinkered with gear while the afternoon wore on. Something was up with Val and Phunuru. They were playing the age old (in this case high altitude) parry and feint male/female dance, then I got it, Phunuru was smitten. Now it all made sense. By plugging my brain to the iPod and following Phinjo's lead of indifference, I kept my tenuous connection to "the zone."

We were pounding the calories more and more but were down to bottom of the barrel freeze dried pseudo food. I daydreamed for my own food bag which held my handpicked food stores anchored by my summit delicacy of Funny Bones. Ever since 1982 when I ran my fastest marathon (2:53), I carb loaded by devouring a box of bones before a big physical event. In 2007 since I didn't summit, others on the hill had enjoyed my chemical-laden delicacy. In 2008 I was ready — I took great pains to pack them in crush proof containers wrapped in duct tape, all for naught. Although I was very lucky to have Monty's stash, I pined for my "bones."

I didn't sleep at all but was on my back all day lazing. We had decided or, I should say the Sherpas did, that we would be leaving at eight p.m., not nine p.m. as previously planned. There were twenty other people in camp going for the top and we wanted to get in front of them and not get stuck at bottlenecks on the route.

In hindsight, I realized I had only thought about the ascent, not the descent. But, at the time it sounded like a sane plan.

Amazingly, like at other tent sites on the mountain, if clear and not windy, it got warm in the thin air in the tent, even at twenty six thousand feet. I was quickly able to dry my gloves, and most importantly, all layers of my boots before May twenty-third got cooler and cooler as the sun set. As this process wended its way, I started to add layers with three hours to go before climbing started. First, I put the down suit back on but only half way. Then I put socks and gloves in my sleeping bag to keep them toasty. Then my hat went over my hoodie, followed by the upper part of my down suit, all the while continuing to pump fluids.

I had gone over my summit gear all afternoon. I would carry two liters of water in my inside insulated down pockets, camera and spare batteries in outside down pockets along with nine energy gels, and in my outside non-insulated pockets I had clear Home Depot safety glasses for protection from blowing ice crystals at night, and glacier goggles for the next morning when the sun was out. In the remaining pocket I stashed my med kit including four tabs of dexamethasone for cerebral edema (brain swelling), and pulmonary edema (lung swelling), the drug of choice for the latter being none other than Viva Viagra itself. These two conditions have killed many a Himalayan Climber and though I deemed it improbable that I would become afflicted, I may be called upon to help others.

In my Wild Things pack, which zips into a tight sleeve for the oxygen bottle, I carried my ski goggles and extra super warm mitts. On the pack I had Kurt's baby shoe clipped to the back and my ice axe in the holder. Within a secret compartment, I had two flags to fly at the summit, one featured "Chiropractic At The Top of the World," and the other was — top secret.

At seven p.m. I started to open the chemical hand warmers and, like the rest of the trip, couldn't get them to fire up. Seems they need oxygen to activate and leave it to me to be in the world's worst place for that element. I finally got one to engage and pressed it in to my right glove. My socks warmed to perfection in my sleeping bag and after putting them on I slid my inner boots in the bag to warm. The balaclava went on as I opened an energy gel and squeezed it into the hopper with a last half-liter of water. Things were really picking up steam in a slow motion, hypoxic, not-too-bright-four-year-old kind of way.

I was thrilled to be at the South Col of Mt. Everest and became teary-eyed when I thought of all the people who helped me to be there. *Within an hour I will be leaving for the top-of-the-World,"* I thought incredulously. I could barely believe it. As I re-read my journal to write this account two years later, I can still barely believe it happened and remain very, very thankful, especially because I lived to tell the tale.

The activity level outside the tent reached fever pitch all of a sudden, as I pulled on inner boots, unzipped the tent flap and then pulled on the outer boots carefully, making sure to prevent creases which could cause blisters. Any and every glitch which can be prevented or avoided is huge at altitude, and especially on the last leg of Everest. I dragged myself out the tent door into the night and clicked on my headlamp. The tent town was abuzz with head lamp beams cris-crossing the Col like light sabers. *I need to be a Jedi Knight at least for the next eighteen hours,* I mumbled to myself.

I had my pack on and affixed with oxygen apparatus but was having a heck of a time getting one crampon on, as I had allowed the strap to become encased in bullet proof ice in the tent vestibule and it wouldn't pass through the buckle. Count that as a glitch which could have and should have been prevented. Luckily, Justin Merle, an IMG guide who summitted with his clients Jaroslaw and Dean earlier that day, took the bull by the horns, did his guide magic and pulled the strap through without muss or fuss.

There was nothing left to do except climb Mt. Everest. Totally freakin' unreal was all I could think. The first part travelling over the flat Col was an exercise in avoiding garbage, from decades' old rusted cans to brand new, 2008 abandoned food and equipment. There were brand new carabiners and other hardware that in any other situation I would have grabbed as "booty." Even in my hepped-up state I remembered thinking, *wow, this is the only part of this mountain that is not absolutely pristine and in fact it is absolutely filthy.* Were it not such a low snow year I wouldn't have noticed the half of it.

The grade started to increase as we approached the low end of the triangular face, so named for its, get this, triangular shape. Val rushed in front to film us as we walked by and I marveled at how she had so much energy. It was me and Phi, Mike Hamill and Dasonam, Serge, Ryan and Panuru, and Val and Phunuru on our little team.

I entered an altered state of existence where I was encased in a sarcophagus of down suit and hood, face covered by the oxygen mask leaving only my eyes exposed. I was climbing in a yellow goose-down bourkha. Communication was impossible except to shout at very close range. The entire world existed in the six-foot beam of light coming from my squash.

Hours rolled by and we kept climbing up, up, up. Sometimes I sensed others around me and came to a standstill, most of the time I was quite alone. At one point, I lifted a leg to get on the other side of the rope and I inadvertently booted Mike Hamill, square in the chest, crampons first. Twelve, sharpened two-inch spikes right to the chest. I screamed an apology that I knew he wouldn't hear and was waved on. I just kept going. Days later at Base Camp, I apologized again, but he had no idea what I was talking about so, evidently, it was somebody else (or it was Elvis).

IMG Everest Expedition
Dispatch #40 May 23, 2008
IMG leader Mark Tucker just got off the radio with the climbers, who report that Val and Phunuru, Tim and Phinjo, Hamill and Dasonam, Ryan and Passang, and Serge and Panuru left the Col at 8:16 p.m. They left early to get ahead of the bulk of the climbers — there are only a few ahead of them. Weather is good. Remaining in support on the South Col are Ang Karma, Datenji, and Tshewang Lendu. We'll keep you posted on their progress.
Eric Simonson End of Dispatch

I sensed huge voids on either side but my beam of light revealed nothing. Hours into the climb I witnessed a diamond sky reveal itself in glorious fashion. Fourth of July fireworks in Wickford Harbor couldn't begin to be as dramatic. Some parts of the climbing route were very steep and others were straight up. At one point I glanced to my right and saw a dead body completely uncovered except for his head embedded in ice. He had a blue one-piece suit festooned with Italian logos, presumably those of his sponsors. His cramponed boots lay gently on the snow and ice. Except for his head, he had the body habitus of a man just taking a breather ... perhaps that was exactly what he did in his last minutes. In quick succession, two more bodies. There must be a hollow or a jet stream wind deflection which allowed the bodies to stay where they were in that God-forsaken place and not be blown into Tibet.

In 2007 the gossip at Asian Trekking's bakery at Base Camp was that Scott Fisher's (famed American climber and guide who passed away in a storm in 1996) body had become visible in the ice that year. I presumed that he was one of the deceased I observed.

Suddenly after pulling up on the ascender and stomping steps in the steep terrain of a snow gulley, I found myself in a flurry of frantic activity. I realized that this flat place, with about ten people shouting into radios in multiple tongues, was the Balcony at 27,500 feet. A woman asked me if she could get in front of me as she had clients to take care of, and I recognized her as Lydia Bradey from New Zealand, the first woman to summit Everest sans supplemental oxygen.

I quickly popped a GU and took a long slurp of water as Phi took it upon himself to change my oxygen bottle. Was he cool or what? I really wanted to do this myself in order to make absolutely sure I was in charge of my destiny, but he started the process and damned if I wasn't going to let him finish. The wind picked up tremendously as the balcony was quite exposed. I wrestled my clear glasses out of my pocket but then realized I had broken them. *Screw it*, I thought, *just keep going.* I stashed the broken parts in my suit as Phi chattered on in Nepali with Ang Jangbu at Base about our timing and progress. We started off.

We may have stopped for five minutes, tops. Same altered existence, for more hours and hours, more alone than together now. At some point Phi's headlamp died and we had to rely on just mine. So glad I changed the batteries at high camp. It was just another thing that could kill you on Everest. If we had no light we would be immobile and could freeze to death. A seemingly innocuous event like losing a glove would also be fatal. The hypothermia would infiltrate your body slowly shutting it down and eventually ending your life.

I asked Phi what time it was as I couldn't read my watch. He said, "It's three a.m." It was May 24, 2008 and Phi and I had been on the go for seven hours since leaving high camp. At that point, I had not slept in twenty-four hours, and except for the eight hours at Camp Four, we had been climbing steadily in the death zone that whole time. Minutes later, Phinjo motioned ahead and said, "South Summit". I followed his gesture with my gaze and before me rose an immense vertical feature, that of the lesser summit of the top of the world.

The South Summit sat at 28,800 feet and was approximately two hours from the true summit. It was also the site of much sadness and death, poignantly described in Krakauer's *Into Thin Air*. This was a common turn-around point for climbers too exhausted to continue and later we learned that Ryan and Serge made the courageous and intelligent call to do just that.

My hands had been cold but not numb. One of my chemical warmers was working and I alternated warming fingers. When safety cord was attached to the line, I took those few seconds of safety to slap my deadened digits against my thigh to keep the circulation going, alternating hands on the cold metal of carabiner or jumar was important too. Mercifully, my feet remained warm.

I couldn't help thinking of Rob Hall, Doug Hansen and Andy Harris who met their ends at or near this area. We began the short descent to the cat walk between the South Summit and the Hillary Step where the exposure was tremendous. It was just a feeling of immense voids on either side. And even though I couldn't see beyond my torch light, my heart was in my throat with fear. This was the major leagues.

The catwalk took brass balls (or brass ovaries). This was the feature that filled me with loathing just hearing about it in 2007. We clambered across and came to an area of relative safety amongst the rocks and at this point I realized with a start, *Holy hell, we might summit in pitch black!*

The sky was brightening ever so slowly as we continued our ascent, and I mimed to Phi my intention to stop for a drink as we had taken no nourishment for hours since the Balcony. He didn't react at all. I took this to mean that the terrain must be more dangerous than I'd realized and I set off after him. Phi screamed over a now rising, very cold wind, "Hillary Step." I was just flabbergasted ... gobsmacked was more like it, at my whereabouts. I was so thankful to be there at mountaineering's most fabled feature, but simultaneously "shitting a brick and a wooden nickel" with chest constricting fear. We ascended, but found it difficult to locate the year's fixed rope (installed a few days earlier by our friends Dawa and Danuru Sherpa) among all the tattered rope remnants of years past. Some were rotted to nothing more than an old clothes line's frayed core. As we scaled a rock trough and climbed upwards, we had a tricky dance on a downward slanted table-like rock where the crampons scraped like fingernails on a blackboard. At this point we had a 7,000 foot void directly below us. I nearly spotted.

"Fear – an energy source designed to increase performance."
— Laird Hamilton

Except for the significant hazards, mental and physical, of exposure and altitude, the difficulty wasn't huge for the Step. If this pitch were at home in the White Mountains, Rob Scott and I wouldn't have roped up for it. At the Hillary Step on May 24, 2008, nearly five and a half miles in the sky, I was shaking like Palmer the pup passing a peach pit.

We just climbed the Hillary Step, I kept repeating. With forty-five minutes to the summit of heavily corniced but relatively safe snow slopes, I realized for the first time since leaving Base Camp that, *I just might summit Mt. Everest! I might just summit this thing!*

With so many potential things to derail your climb or even kill you, it just hadn't occurred to me since setting out that I would actually summit. Almost on cue, the sky brightened. It was a sign ... that I would survive.

An arctic wind picked up and penetrated my down one-piece. In a few minutes two descending climbers came into view and I fist bumped Phunuru and Val Hovland. She was one strong climbing chick, to summit in such good style while filming periodically. She also has the significant baggage of frostbite damaged feet from a disastrous climb of Shishapangma in Tibet, two years previous with Monty Smith, of unstoppable bloody nose fame. Monty had stumps for pinkie fingers as a lifelong reminder of the same climb.

Shuffling up the snow slopes, Mike Hamill and Dasonam were suddenly next to us and we screamed our congratulations over the wind as they dropped below. Twenty minutes of head down, focused slogging, while intently staring at the snow to make sure I wasn't stepping on a fracturing snow cornice, brought us to a sudden standstill. There was no place higher to go. We were at the top. We were at the top of the world! We were the tallest knuckleheads in the world!

An ephemeral pile of prayer flags, a single Poisk Oxygen bottle, a framed picture of the Dalai Lama ... and Phinjo Sherpa and Tim Warren were ... the top of the world! It was 5:11a.m. Nepal time on 5/24/2008. Standing there, six feet tall, my eyes gazed at the curve of the earth below me from 29,041 feet.

IMG Everest Expedition

Dispatch #41 May 23, 2008

IMG leader Mark Tucker reports that the IMG team reached the summit at sunrise and have now all started their descent. Congrats to Val and Phunuru, Tim and Phinjo, Mike and Dasonam, and Passang Sherpa. Ryan and Serge turned back from near the South Summit and are now at the Col.

Eric Simonson

End of Dispatch.

"There is no passion to be found living small, in settling for a life that is less than the one you are capable of living."

— **Nelson Mandela**

Chapter Six

"Nature never overlooks a mistake or makes the smallest allowance for ignorance."
— Aldus Huxley

"Hey Jangbu", yelled Phinjo into the radio, "We have to turn around". "But why," hissed Jangbu with alarm. "Cause there is no place higher in the world to go, hah", said Phinjo.

Phinjo and I cried with heaving sobs as we hugged tightly on the summit, the tears instantly freezing to our cheeks in the minus twenty-five degree air. Phi wrestled off his pack and reverently pulled out a kata scarf that he had painstakenly printed with our names and the date in English and Nepali. I thought, *Cool, that is gonna look smokin' in a frame back in my office,* but alas, it was destined to be affixed to the summit for good karma. Like prayer flags, the good ju-ju was intended to go way beyond the expedition. As the scarf's threads inevitably became airborne in the severe winds, it was believed that they travel to all corners of the earth, spreading positive energy and good karma. Phi lashed the kata to a strand of prayer flags snapping violently in the wind. The already brutal wind was intensifying and I noticed the cold permeating my body, most notably the quadriceps of both legs just where the tops of my overboots ended. I was frozen to the core the second I stopped moving. The cold seemed to add fifty pounds of weight to my already stressed frame. I didn't dare remove my gloves as I rummaged for my camera , knowing that I would lose my fingers to frostbite if I touched anything metallic in the incalculable wind chill. Phi appeared ice indifferent.

As I removed the tiny Canon camera from my outside insulated pocket I was stunned to see it entombed in ice. Evidently dripping saliva from my breathing apparatus had seeped into the pocket and had frozen the camera into a brick. I couldn't believe my good luck as I hit the "on" button and it came to life, needing only a little persuasion to open the lens cover. I was doubly glad I had put in fresh batteries at the South Col. I took shots of Phi alone and Phi with his kata. He took some of me wrestling the two flags I had brought for the event. In the relentless wind, I was hoping that the messages would remain clear in photos.

As soon as we radioed Tuck and Jangbu to check in, it was past time to go down. The cold and wind were too intense to force water and energy gel into my body, and my exposed cheeks were so wind-chilled I could no longer speak. Two other climbers came up as we saddled up our packs, smoothed our oxygen tubes and headed down. Altogether, we were on the summit seven to ten minutes. The wind was about twenty miles an hour steady, with higher gusts, and the temperature was estimated by others that day as minus twenty five degrees F. It was a perfect summer day ... on Mars.

"It's a big mountain, and me...not so big."
— Dr. Tim Warren

With one spiked boot in Nepal and one in occupied Tibet, Phi and I started down climbing Mt. Everest's Southeast Ridge, realizing full well that at the summit of any mountain you are, at best, half-way home. By far, the most scary and dangerous time is the descent. Nowhere is that more true than at Everest and the thirteen other 8,000 meter peaks. We now had to get down fast to preserve our fingers and toes, and our lives. Fifty-six percent of deaths on Everest have occurred while descending from the summit. Seventeen percent of deaths occurred after turning around short of the summit. Out of every ten successful climbs, one ends in death. These scary stats were never far from my mind as I dedicated one-hundred-percent of body and soul to safely descend each step.

Often there is a psychological let-down of attention post summit, sometimes leading to a missed clip on a rope or a trip on a protruding rock with a crampon. The debilitating lack of oxygen pressure reeks havoc on accurate decision-making and climbing technique and the more time spent in the death zone, the greater the risk of cerebral edema, which routinely kills Himalayan climbers in their tracks. One moment lucid, the next comatose.

Bathed in the full light of day we could not escape the gut-tightening exposure as we descended past broken rock and corniced overhangs. We had been running on pure adrenaline, having digested the last measly hundred calories of energy gel many hours previous. It was just too dangerous to stop for a swig of water and more GU.

I couldn't speak for Phi, but I began to feel mightily wasted as we dispatched the "easy" snow slopes and came to the top of the Hillary

Step. The constant muscle ache of fatigue was building. At first we made good progress, but then we had to pass two slowly ascending climbers. It was impossible to keep clipped on the fixed rope as there was no room to safely pass. Time was ticking by and the exhausted climbers, still an hour from the summit, were bent over at the waist with heaving lungs and completely oblivious to anything but their own suffering.

Finally, I followed Phi's lead and simply grabbed a handful of old ropes and literally swung down Tarzan style past the last guy. There was 7,000 feet of nothing to my right and 10,000 feet of nothing to my left.

A slip in any direction would have been our deaths due to the fact we were not clipped in. In fifteen years of climbing, I had never taken such risks on any pitch on any climb, and I chastised myself firmly. I was horrified with my behavior, but it was the only way to get around these dudes who barely moved. In that moment I opted for speed of descent rather than safe climbing technique. I got away with it, that time. The joke was that if you do fall, you choose the 10,000 foot side because you'll live longer. Ha,Ha.

We moved with better speed for about thirty seconds having picked a good safe line. We found cracks for our crampons in the stone and good hand holds in the jagged rocks above us. This time we were clipped in.

We were at the sphincter-puckering down sloping rock of the Hillary Step with Phi in front when he snapped his head back and made eye contact with me. I couldn't read his meaning, and we couldn't converse in the screaming wind, but as I caught up to him and peered around the corner, my heart was instantly in my throat and epinephrine surged, skyrocketing my heart rate. A painfully slow train of ten climbers, barely moving a muscle, were ascending this most exposed part of the climb. There was nothing to do, we were trapped halfway up and halfway down the Hillary Step, stuck in the middle of an exhausted humanity operating on nothing but desire and muted messages from their reptilian brains.

Phi and I intertwined arms as close as possible to the rock wall on our left and I shoved one crampon halfway onto a three inch shelf of rock, and made sure our safety loops were clipped. We clung to each other and to the vertical rock spine like spiders to a web. We didn't move. Minutes dragged, at one point two seemingly strong climbers tried to squeeze by us and essentially pushed and pulled a tiny member of the Nepali Women's Team up the rock as her head lolled to one side.

As these two "handlers" placed her boots on the rock and pulled her up, it didn't appear that mentally she was on the planet.

Glancing ahead, I was stunned to see people on the South Summit trying to get an exhausted climber up on his feet. I had a ringside, albeit immovable, seat to a horrifying spectacle. This guy was fighting to stand up, failing, trying to crawl, failing again. His friends tried to hoist him up with rope, at which they succeeded, only to have the man topple over in a face plant without moving his hands to protect himself. I was flabbergasted by what I was seeing. *My God, we are smack dab in the middle of Into Thin Air part two,* I screamed into my mask. I was six inches from Phi's left ear and he couldn't hear a word.

Here was bowled over, shocked, scared-to death madness, all in the most dangerously exposed and oxygen-less environment on earth. People seemed out-of-control and completely unaware of it. *Did I look as terrible coming up,* I thought.

I was getting "sewing-machine-leg," climber speak for muscles giving way under too much exertion, so I hopped and cajoled my free leg to take the place on the three-inch shelf that the other leg had occupied for nigh on fifteen minutes. I couldn't help but jar Phi a bit from his perch as I performed cramponed gymnastics stuck to near vertical rock at 28,800 feet. To his credit Phi complained not a whit, just another day at the office for him (window office…with view).

Suddenly, I noticed Phi was extricating himself while studying the throng below. I realized, without exchanging words, that he wanted to bolt for it, and I was certainly going with him. The next instant, when the next climber, heading up towards us, collapsed on his heaving chest over his ice axe to rest, Phi was off like the wind. The two of us cut deftly between two climbers, seized decrepit ropes, and taking Everest-sized chances, lowered ourselves down the Step – not protected. *This is why there are no dead bodies up here,* I snorted, *they swan-dive for miles ending up as frozen ooze.*

The precipices were beguiling and terrible. *No mistakes now, focus on every step and every clip, focus on every little movement, stay alive,* I repeated over and over. *Focus, focus, focus.* Finally down at the catwalk, we scampered across to the South Summit. Slogging dog-tired up the thirty-five feet to the pinnacle, I whined, *I don't want go up anymore, I just want go down"* There was no sign of the out-of-his-mind-and-body climber.

The route was a completely new experience since it was pitch-black on the ascent four hours previous. Even had it not been nighttime, all trails looked completely different in opposite direction of travel.

Phi didn't stop for a second after going over the top. He just motored his way down. The sun was beating down with no cloud visible, and still I shivered in the gusty wind. My hands alternated being frozen so I changed the hand used for climbing paraphernalia and reinstated my thigh slapping and finger curling routine. The fatigue really started to build. My legs were feeling pretty fair, but my arms were so wasted it took super-human effort and concentration to apply the safety loop attached to my climbing harness to the fixed rope. Once mindless habit, now I had to will my fingers to attach safety 'biner to the rope at each anchor and to arm wrap (or arm 'rap', short for rappel), this procedure, along with my twenty-four two-inch spikes were my only tenuous connections to life.

We descended mindlessly for hours and I constantly changed the arm muscles being used, as I had lost the strength necessary to move my fingers, forearms and upper arms due to fatigue, decreased blood flow and low oxygen concentrations. I used the fingers on one hand to force the fingers of the other to grasp the steel snap-link. My fingers had become wooden and claw-like, as if they were prosthetics. I used a cadre of rope friction techniques to descend, including the arm wrap using both arms, and angel rappels. I repeated my mantra from other climbs and hikes when I was knackered with fatigue: *the trail never ends*. Strangely, these words always gave me solace and hope.

Although I was freezing, my forehead and cheeks had become badly sunburned in the troposphere, the altitude at which 747's routinely fly. I had not thought to apply zinc oxide upon leaving for the summit the previous night at eight p.m. Now it just wasn't safe to stop. Sauron, the dark lord, was directing his legions to disintegrate my Anglo-Saxon epidermis.

I was aware that little mistakes such as not applying sunscreen, accumulate, and increase the chances of an Everest emergency. Once again, I rededicated myself to safety.

The rubber oxygen mask was rubbing me raw in places not already sunburned, especially under my eyes and over the temples. With each labored respiration the apparatus ground into the wounds like sandpaper. My wrap-around glacier glasses were fogging badly with moist air escaping the oxygen mask. I started to get angry. When I tried to vent one body part another was chilled. I was getting upset. I elicited a moan and an epithet with each step.

To add to my accumulating irritation, Phi seemed to be taking off from me. He was twenty yards ahead and not waiting. I mumbled angrily, and occasionally loudly, while generally bearing ill will to myself and the world, when two climbers came down behind me. I guessed they'd had enough because one of them, (turned out to be Walter Laserer, the Austrian mountain guide with his client whom I had met at Camp One several days previous) said, "Hey man, you summitted right?" and "You are with IMG right?" Still not recognizing him with my altitude addled mind, I answered affirmatively. "Dude, great place for a photo", he said cheerily as he motioned for my camera. We snapped a couple of frames and Laserer and client were quickly off like the proverbial new bride's pajamas.

As I continued my solitary painful plod downhill, the thought occurred to me that I never would have stopped if not for Walter's shaking my tree. I was unaware of the amazing world that I was at the top of, but was intent on moaning and groaning. Due to fear, I was in my own head and oblivious to what surrounded me: a pristine day, the snow, ice and rock of the worlds' biggest mountain under my boots, Kanchenjunga, the third highest peak in the world, Lhotse, the worlds' fourth and Makalu, the worlds' fifth were my neighbors. And, I was, for the moment, safe. I felt better because I had some human contact from someone who was enjoying the experience. Walter was upbeat and it was contagious. I started to anticipate surviving to Camp Four.

Tears flowed suddenly as I realized I would never see this scene again. More tears came as I realized how lucky I was and how thankful I was. *I am never going to be here again so enjoy the moment, I murmured.*

"Commonplace miracle: that so many commonplace miracles happen...A miracle, just take a look around: the World is everywhere."
— Wislawa Szymborska

"Sieze the day and put the least possible trust in tomorrow."
— Horace

All we ever have is the "now" — the past is a memory and the future a dream. All that exists is right-this-second. I remembered an exchange in Dan Millman's book *The Peaceful Warrior* "Where are you?" asks the teacher, "Here" says the student. "What time is it?" the teacher asks again, "Now" replies the student. I repeated this passage while standing stock-still at 27,800 feet completely wasted with fatigue.

After clipping into the next anchor, I sat on my haunches and took a moment, the first real mental and physical "break" on that amazing day. I reminded myself that I was right "here" and the time was "now." I was in a beautiful, fascinating place and was having an extraordinary experience and I wouldn't miss it, I reminded myself to live in the moment and be aware. I wanted to etch the scene into my memory bank. On the other hand I realized I must not linger as a lack of focus can and would kill me.

It's the Yin and Yang of an Everest climb, success and death can occupy the same moment. I vowed to stop my bitching, whining and anger at myself and Phi, and live in the moment while redoubling my focus on safely descending. My entire existence became wrapped in taking the next safe step, all spikes in the ice, safety loop secure, arm wrap on fixed rope, with minimal slack. I refused to allow my thoughts to linger on pain and fatigue. Those thoughts, as with sea-level, would not aid my survival.

> *"When we live in awareness it is easy to see miracles everywhere."*
>
> — Anon

I discovered after years of practice that one of my favorite things about climbing was that no room existed for extraneous cerebral subject matter when in a precarious situation. It's a very simple life, do what you must to keep yourself alive for another few seconds, then, worry about the next few seconds, then the next. No time to think about paying bills, mowing the grass, or getting in a fight with your honey.

I realized then why Phi's behavior had had me ripped, it was because I was completely and utterly terrified. This was a revelation at that moment and I was amazed at the obviousness. I wasn't ruminating on the myriad events that could potentially smite me down but the possibilities must have been lurking in the la-la-land of my subconscious.

I rousted myself from introspective reverie as I had big work to do: stay alive. I gazed down on the Balcony at 27,500 feet, but it seemed never to appear any closer no matter how hard I worked. The switchbacks of rope were never ending although my focus was renewed. I realized that to eat this elephant, it would take one bite at a time — the same way I got up there.

Finally, I met up with Phi at the queen bed-sized resting spot of the Balcony. I removed my pack and plopped exhaustedly down. Mike Hamill and Dasonam were gearing up to go down. I had always gotten a kick out of Dasonam, because he was a little overweight with cherubic face and wore round wire rimmed spectacles. However, the unassuming exterior belied a powerful athlete — he has summitted Everest *ten* times.

At the rest stop I found that my words to Phi were still sharp and whiny so I realized I was still not in the moment. I was still selfishly in my own head, still focused on my own pain with no thought to his. I looked him in the eyes and apologized. I told him I was deathly afraid and had been for the bulk of the previous twenty four hours. He nodded, and accepted my apology in wordless understanding. He had been "there" many times before, not just physically but experientially. He has been a devout Buddhist and an accomplished professional Himalayan mountaineer for many, many years and he knew "the gig." He knew before I did.

Upon reflection months later, I realized, not surprisingly, that Everest was different on many levels; nothing subtle, no gray areas. In the arena of "fear" on other large mountains I was in a state of low-level "focused fear" while climbing, sometimes for weeks at a time. The majority of time on the "Big E", there was little conscious experience of fear — except for the nearly overwhelming variety experienced on summit day.

I squeezed the double chocolate, caffeine-fortified energy gel with its consistency of cake frosting into my mouth and chased it with a long swig of water. A quick check of my supplies was a bolt-from-the-blue. In our nine hour ascent and three hour descent back to the Balcony, I drank a grand total of one long pull of water and one gel. Not enough to stave off depletion and dehydration while lazing at sea level.

Pre-climb at the South Col, I believed my supply of nine gels and two liters of water would be cutting close to the life/death line. I didn't count on my inability or lack of desire to stop. I chalked my dehydration up to spectacularly exposed terrain and, overwhelming terror. There were just no safe places to stop.

In speaking with my teammates later, in the comfort of *The Rum Doodle* bar in Kathmandu (where Everest summiters eat free for life), I learned that many summiters experienced a variation of the same depleted state. The only explanation was that we ran on another type of fuel on Everest's summit day, a high octane blend of desire, motivation and the ability to endure supreme suffering.

I was not looking forward to the last fifteen hundred foot descent to the relative safety of Camp Four at the South Col. With the wasted state of my upper extremities it was all I could do to affix mask and pack. It was eight a.m. and had been three hours since we stood on the

Earth's highest point and shed our tears. My whole existence that day was a surreal eternity.

I allowed myself one huge luxury with the weather clear in all directions and feeling confident that I would reach camp safely. Having plenty of oxygen, I cranked my flow from three liters per minute to six. I couldn't say that I felt any difference but metabolically it would nourish me on multiple levels. Gazing almost directly below us, I saw our miniature tent city at the South Col and it appeared I could just step out with one big boot and be there.

We started the down climb as a group of four but Mike and Dasonam moved at a quicker pace. Loose rocks constantly broke off the exposed slabs and careened crazily down the steep cliff. Several times we shouted the classic climber warning of "Rock!" or "Ice!" to Mike and Dasonam below us. The projectiles weren't big enough to kill but some could maim. Dasonam was unfazed and never bothered to even turn around.

Within minutes, we descended to the macabre scene of the three dead climbers. Upon arriving at the outstretched body of the one with his head encased in ice but body exposed, we stopped a moment to offer a silent prayer. It bothered me that there we were, almost safe at camp, in perfect weather, so close we could almost reach out and touch our salvation, while next to us lay in eternity our fellow adventurers, dead, with exposed flesh like perfect white porcelain, and doubtless just as hard.

On the descent the whole idea astonished me. Sure, I had signed the same body disposal documents that everyone had in order to get their permits. (Three choices on the mandatory form: 1) If you died on the mountain and if deemed safe to bring your body home for repatriation, this option can cost $50 grand plus. 2) If you died on the mountain and it's safe to bring your body to a local village and have a Buddhist cremation ceremony that will be $20 grand plus. 3) The last option was if you died on the mountain your mates would do their best to deposit your carcass in a crevasse, for free. No brainer – I checked option three) We all knew from multiple books that people die on mountains. And yes, I had had some near misses, and seen dead climbers on other climbs, but this was different. At that point I was sure I would survive the trip but found myself in an ice mausoleum with the (relative) safety of Camp Four less than two hours away in perfect conditions.

"Out of intense complexities, intense simplicities emerge."
— **Winston Churchill**

Where Am I?

Upon reflection months later, I realized both living and non-living had all started with the same goals, motivations, and enthusiasm. Why do some die and some live? This question, in various forms and circumstances, has been bandied about as long as we have peopled the Earth, and it's highly doubtful that I will come up with any cogent answers. In the mountaineering arena in which we played, I suspected that it had most to do with "right motivation."

Decisions, good and bad, are made based on motivation. Are you pressed by monetary considerations, such as keeping sponsors happy, or a feeling that you have to summit, because you have so much dollar value personally invested? Is your self-esteem so wrapped around the project that your attitude is "summit or die trying?" Are you missing home so much that you are pressing the accelerator to the floor? Are time and business constraints forcing poor decision making on the hill?

There have been a couple of cases of suspected "suicide by Everest" where people were so unprepared or made such bad decisions that the only clear conclusion was that they wanted to go out in a blaze of glory. For me, my motivation was simple. Climbing Mt. Everest was something I wanted to do and I thought I could do it. I desired a huge multi-faceted challenge to reveal the outer limits of my potential. I wanted and received a quantum shift in my life. It was as simple as that and as profound as that.

Our journey continued down, and ironically I felt a bit less wasted. Maybe it had something to do with the mantle of fear being raised off my shoulders or just because I had six liters per minute of life-giving oxygen feeding my tissues. The slope began to ease as we emerged from the shooting gallery of falling rocks on the Triangular Face.

As we descended, a young Sherpa with heavy load approached us and seemed confused, he suddenly turned on his heels and descended, then, a hundred yards away he collapsed in the snow. We picked up our pace to get to him, and now he was up and approaching us again. I got in his face and asked him how he was, looking for signs of cerebral or pulmonary edema. He asked for water. Between gulps on my mostly unused water supply, he told us that he was a porter and aspiring summit climber trying to impress his boss (sirdar) by doing extra gear carries. He had gotten confused and dehydrated in the process. He tagged along the last half hour to camp and we saw to it that he got back to his compadres.

It was ten a.m. and we were safe. During the last flat walk to our tents I felt no emotion, just a desire to collapse. It's imperative to drink and eat, but all I wanted to do was pass out. We had been on the go for fourteen hours, and in that time I had drunk only one half liter of water and consumed two energy-gels. I had slept five hours out of the previous fifty.

Suddenly, our Sherpas swarmed about and eased off our packs and untangled us from oxygen tubes. I was led to my tent whereupon I collapsed onto a knee to remove crampons. I stumbled exhaustedly into my tent and started the process of boot removal, first rip the Velcro, then unzip the outer boot and untie the inner laces, then remove outer boot, then pull off inner boot, and repeat. I pulled my pack in and hooked up another oxygen bottle. Damned if I wasn't going to get as much gas in my body as I could, especially since we were at the end of the climbing season and there was plenty for Hahn's group, the only ones left from our team.

As I zippered the tent fly, I noticed that the entire ice floor of the tent vestibule was frozen feces. For all I knew it could be twenty-years-old, as nothing much melted at 26,000 feet. I remembered very little from that point on. I didn't remember eating or drinking, but know that I did. I passed out cold (no pun intended), as did everyone else who climbed that day.

It was still daylight when I awakened and pulled out the satellite phone to call Rose. With a twelve hour time difference I knew it was late, or early, but she answered the phone. The first thing she said before I could get a word in edgewise was, "Honey, you did it!" I was clueless as to what she was talking about since I hadn't told her I summited yet. *How the hell did she already know?* Later, I was able to piece together that when Phi called Mark Tucker and Ang Jangbu from the summit at 5:11 a.m. Nepal-time, one of them e-mailed Eric Simonson in Seattle who crafted an e-mail that went out to Eric's directory including my server at Explorer's Web in New York City. This update on my web site (www.lessonsfromeverest.com) was part of a dispatch to the thousands who followed my climb. Probably by 5:30 a.m. in Nepal and p.m. in America, people knew of our summit and the phone calls and emails were flying, even as we were stumbling down the Hillary Step.

Rose and I spoke for ten minutes till the battery started to peter out. It was hell to hang up, but I could see the end in sight. All I had to do now was get down to Base Camp, safely hike out forty miles, fly to Kathmandu, fly thirty-six hours home and melt in Rose's embrace. Easy! The only positive aspect of our being apart for two and a half months, was that it coincided with Rose's fashion season and we wouldn't have spent much time together even had I not been a couple of continents away.

I stashed the phone inside my fleece third skin to warm the batteries. Next, I called Kurt and he wasn't up, so I left a message that said essentially that I summited and was now safe in camp. As soon as I said "I summited", I became so choked up I couldn't speak.

It was the first time I heard that phrase come out of my mouth and for the very first time I realized it really did happen. It wasn't a dream anymore. It wasn't some airy-fairy pie-in-the-sky statement to people who never believed I could or would do it. I knew then and there that I would be forever changed, not just because I had summited Everest, but that I had done something unequivocal, something nearly impossible for me to fathom. I simply could never again look at the world and my place in it the same way. Challenges and problems would forever more be stacked up against Everest and would lose their power and magnitude. What difficulty could ever look the same when placed on one end of a beam balance, with the grandeur, grace and grit of Chomolungma, Goddess Mother of the World on the other?

Immediately after leaving Kurt's message I felt smarmatose about my statement of being "safe" at the South Col. It's true that in relation to everything above camp to the summit I was safer, but in comparison to any other place in the world short of Waziristan, this had to be just about the most dangerous.

We had existed in the Death Zone, above 25,000 feet, for thirty-six hours and we had twelve more to go before we could escape to areas of slightly lessened danger to our brain cells. I decided not to call in a new message to Kurt with this revelation, I just re-dedicated myself to safely descending to Camp Two the next day and to the total safety of Base Camp the day after that. The death of the Swiss climber three days previous and fifty feet from our tent, cemented in my mind that it was no place to do any ra-ra-shish-boom-ba. I passed out quickly and was dead to the world with my oxygen tube attached, and felt not a thing till I awoke at five a.m.

Wow, am I wasted or what, was my first thought followed by, *oh man, I have to get down the Lhotse Face to Camp Two in one piece today.* We would bypass Camp Three on the way down, just stopping to grab gear and inhale calories. I was nervous as always before a climb, but more so because I was thrashed from the exertion and environment of the previous days. I was bone tired, even though by my calculation, I had passed out for the bulk of the previous nineteen hours.

I vaguely remembered, in my catatonic state, that Val had some eye problems from the descent. Various radio calls ensued with Base Camp and HRA, before Hahn, at 24,500 feet at that moment, diagnosed it as eye trauma from blowing ice crystals during our nocturnal ascent. She was relieved obviously because it could have been something significantly more serious, like a high altitude stroke. It's a very tenuous connection to life, this high altitude climbing business, and I for one was damn ready, mentally if not physically, to vamanos.

With unsteady bobbing and weaving, I crawled out of the tent with all my top of the world possessions, and with new and different focus turned my gaze to the summit route. Realizing with sadness that I would never be there again in person, I allowed myself the five minute luxury of a meditative connection to the summit experience before leaving it all behind. I hated to admit it but I also had the fleeting feeling of disappointment that the great mountain had succumbed to my assault. Almost immediately after that reflection, I stuffed the idea down deep inside, as I definitely didn't want to go there. Was my self-esteem showing a fatigue fracture? Was it the inevitable contemplative ending for a many-years' long goal attained?

We left the South Col at seven a.m. and scraped our way down the disintegrating down-sloping stone shelves of the Geneva spur to the long snow traverse to the Yellow Band. We ran into Hahn and his group on their way up. Congrats were offered and accepted. My eyes got watery as Dave relayed that everyone at camp was totally stoked that I, in particular, was successful on my second seeking of the Holy Grail of mountaineering.

My intention was to be a helpful, supportive non-obtrusive asset to my climbing brethren on this expedition. I knew I had been successful on all fronts when Dave told that story while five of us chatted, attached to safety cordage at 25,500 feet.

I hadn't always had Dave's respect. In 2007 he stirred up stuff with me at Camp One regarding the ruse of my using wrong radio etiquette with Tuck. That changed this year when, after the first acclimatization cycle, I remarked at dinner that the icefall route seemed easier than the previous year and he broke in and said "No, the route is always hard, you are different". Stupefied, I couldn't even respond to the compliment. Dave has the most non-Sherpa ascents of Everest at twelve and has no remotely close competitors with twenty-seven ascents of Vinson Massiv in Antarctica.

As we continued the descent, the sunshine became intense, but since it was around twenty degrees, I was thankfully not overheating in my down suit with overloaded pack.

I was descending alone when little by little I realized that I couldn't stop staring at my shadow in the snow. With the angle of the morning sun, my shadow was to my left the majority of the time. I was mesmerized. I simply could not stop staring at the dynamic, strangely hypnotic sight. It was fascinating.

Slipping my safety loop at an anchor in the ice and arm rappelling down the fixed rope with stumbling feet while obsessively focusing at my shadow was no way to safely descend any mountain. I suddenly felt totally wasted. My arm and leg muscles felt sodden, water-logged. It was nearly an out-of-body experience. I had the feeling of watching a slow-motion movie, only the show was my undulating shadow in the snow. I snapped to attention. It occurred to me that this was not remotely good, in fact could kill me. This could be a symptom of cerebral edema and possibly end-stage.

In cerebral edema the brain swells inside the skull, where there is only so much extra space, sometimes squeezing down the foramen magnum and compressing the medulla oblongata which houses the respiratory and cardiac centers. If swelling persists, a climber can be dead before he hits the ground. Beginning symptoms are not unlike inebriation, in fact, sobriety tests are administered to document a suspected case. In all cases, it's fatal unless you lose altitude double quick. I had carried four milligrams of dexamethasone tablets all the way to the summit and although they were still in my top pocket, I wasn't ready to self-diagnose. At the time I didn't see the irony – seemingly safely descending post-summit, but with a rapidly swelling brain I could die any second. After a seventy day expedition where I had harnessed my brain power so successfully, my brain might actually do me in. I flipped open my mountaineering watch, the altitude read 25,280 feet.

Phinjo was way ahead and it would get lost in translation even if I told him my concerns, so I stopped at the next anchor to try to bring a halt to the horror. I traced my oxygen tube as far as I could, no twists in it that I could tell. Next, I checked my mask. *Unbelievable,* I croaked. The sewn-on hood of my down suit had become adhered to the ambient air intake and was cutting my oxygen flow to near nil, resulting in my being dumb as a box-o-rocks. *Whew, dodged that bullet,* I thought, and instantly my lungs expanded with life-giving gas. I berated myself for another mistake made.

We arrived at the top of the crumbling Yellow Band and like the trip up, my gloves were etched deeply with ice and nearly useless to grab hold of the rope. To this day, I have no clue why I didn't grab my figure-eight rappel device and go over the lip backwards for safety, but I didn't, and I nearly met my maker. The only viable explanation for this unforgivable misstep was that I was still dangerously under the influence of cerebral edema.

I was clipped in, of course, but as I went over the lip and committed my body weight to the rope I started to slide due to my ice-encrusted gloves. I tried to brake myself by stabbing my crampons on the rock and ice vertical wall, but if I applied too much pressure I knew I would launch myself out into space. They would find my body, as it was attached to the fixed rope, but it would be a nasty sight. Even if I lived through that potential fall, no one could rescue me with two broken legs at 25,000 feet. In fits-and-starts I was able to slowly lower myself to the snow below the Band, using up valuable strength.

There was no cavalry to come to the rescue, and that's exactly the way it's supposed to be. The long and short of it was that for the third time since the summit descent, I was the poster boy for sorry, unsafe amateur climbing and, like the ascent on this same spot, left me shaken to the core. The Yellow Band, both up and down, was the technical crux of the entire Everest climb for me. Who would have thunk it? No one else, to my knowledge, has ever had an epic at this Everest feature, it's always either above this point or below. My mistakes were accumulating.

Finally, Camp Three was visible below us and we gradually reeled it in, pulled over and got the "pigs" off our backs. I was toast physically, but hoovered more food and drink into the gullet while repacking gear. Off with the down suit and on with Gore-Tex and fleece for the last stretch of climbing down the monumental Lhotse Face to Two. The familiar total wasting of my arms, forearms and hands slowed my progress downhill to a labored, shuffling gear check and double-check ritual. My decisions and safety technique seemed focused, but I was losing control of my body. It simply didn't have much more to give. The "fun-o-meter" was pegged at the lowest setting.

Again, I was furious at myself for not rapping off a couple of vertical ice cliffs and therefore burning energy that I sorely needed. Not to mention the fact that my safety decisions were becoming increasingly suspect. A heavy cloud cover had crept up valley and enveloped the entire Lhotse Face for most of the down climbing which stifled the burning rays of the Death Star. At last some good news.

Hours passed. I finally caught up with Phinjo and told him of my plans to rappel the remaining steep sections of the Face. He looked at me funny for a second and politely agreed. It was then that I glanced around in the swirling mist and laughed out loud. We were already down! In the lost visibility we had cranked down the entire Lhotse

Where Am I?

Face and I didn't even know it. Phi must have thought I was smoking crack.

A safe, easy, and happy one hour stroll down 500 feet to Camp Two and a home cooked meal of dahl-bat followed. I passed out cold for the remainder of the afternoon and didn't leave the tent till the next day when we prepared for the final mental and physical hurdle, the very last trip through the icefall, number twenty for me over both years.

I didn't want to jinx myself, but the icefall was the last thing that could kill me on Everest, unless of course I was crushed by rampaging skin-head yaks on ecstasy in a Khumbu Valley mosh pit.

Three hours after leaving Camp Two at six a.m. on 5/26/08 we removed our spikes at the now familiar crampon point and exhaustedly trudged the last ten minutes across a running-with-melt-water, disintegrating Base Camp. For years I had dreamed and meditated about that moment — summit and safe return.

No bands played, no fanfare, just Mark Tucker waiting for me outside the communications tent with three radios chirping in his ears, and, busting-my-beans, said "Well, you got that monkey off your back."

The cook staff Sherpas came out, congratulated us, and smilingly offered a round of orange Fantas. It was the best tasting, most satisfying liquid that has ever crossed my lips.

Dispatch: Summit and Safe Return
May 26, 2008

Sorry it's been awhile. I can't talk about the last forty-eight hours yet … it's too surreal. I am journaling and will share when I can stay awake for more than a few minutes. I got to the safety of Base Camp a few hours ago, totally spent. Actually, I have been totally spent for days. I have been where humans are just not supposed to be and the corpses are in plain sight as a reminder. As for me, I have all my fingers and toes, have lost a few brain cells, but the remaining ones are smarter. Talk soon, Love, Dr. Tim

End of Dispatch

"Where am I? Here. What time is it? Now."
— **Dan Millman**

Epilogue:
Seven Steps To the Top

*"My mission on earth is to recognize the void – inside
and outside of me – and fill it."*
— Rabbi Menahem

My Everest experience had given me a great gift and I wanted to share it. I realized that mountain climbing was not inherently high on the average person's agenda of most important things-to-do checklist. In fact, my favorite alpine oriented book title is Lionel Terray's *Conquistadors of the Useless*.

In the years since returning from the "Big E", I have had the pleasure of giving dozens of slide presentations all over the country. In the first six months the talks were hard to give for two reasons: first, I could almost not quite believe it had really happened and second, I lost composure and became teary-eyed (proving that it had actually happened).

But with each recitation I was developing a deeper understanding of the lessons I had learned from the expeditions. I was able to objectively compare and contrast the "successful" year from the "unsuccessful," and from the initial pie-in-the-sky idea to successful arrival to Base Camp with all appendages intact. From the beginning, I realized that Everest, and specifically an attempt to climb it, was a great metaphor for life and the struggles we all face as we negotiate our way through the journey of life. Finding meaning, doing the work, enjoying the ride, experiencing hope and thankfulness and finally, like Maslow's pinnacle: awareness. As a result, my lectures developed into teaching these tenets with Everest as backdrop.

I experienced no particular satisfaction in the ten minutes spent buffeted by the wind at 29,035 feet with teeth chattering away in mind numbing cold, nor did I expect to. But as with other lofty peaks attained, the satisfaction has grown every day since. Everest was different, however. The experiences were somehow of a deeper nature, and in the ensuing years have progressively etched deeper still, into the DNA of my soul, if such a substance indeed exists.

I experienced the determination, confidence, and inherent power of the right mission. I reveled in the hard work necessary to fulfill that mission. I encountered a great journey with fascinating people in an astounding place, with breathtaking vistas in all directions. From the valley of despair on a solitary hike in 2008, I discovered a wondrous feeling of utter contentment and serenity (hope) in one eureka moment. I understood then and there probably with a not-so-bright look on my face, that all that was needed to continue any quest was the tiniest shred of hope. In the biggest physical and mental challenge of my life I discovered that thankfulness was a necessary ingredient. Finally, I found that all we truly have is the present, the right now. The Gift. Awareness.

"Every moment comes to you pregnant with a divine purpose. Once you do with it as you please, it plunges into eternity, to remain forever what you made it."
— Fulton J. Sheen

SEVEN STEPS TO THE TOP OF YOUR WORLD
Step One: "What's your Everest?"
Step Two: "Love your work."
Step Three: "Enjoy the ride, because life is the ride."
Step Four: "Hope: a shred is all you need."
Step Five: "Thank your way to the top."
Step Six: "All that exists is this instant, be aware."
Step Seven: "Find a new Everest."

Afterword

"Twenty years from now you will be more disappointed by things you didn't do than by things you did."
— Mark Twain

OK, I stand corrected. In fact, let me be clear, there are places in Lobuche, Nepal that really suck. You see, I had never actually stayed in town there. Twice I had camped for days in the yak pasture hinterlands. Many times I had admired the meandering stream and cute ponies as I huffed and puffed my way to or from Base Camp. Eighteen-year-old son Kurt and I both knew we were in trouble as soon as Suchille Sherpa led us through the rudimentary front door of a nameless windblown teahouse in April 2010.

The air was poisoned by a leaky kerosene stove. The floor was poorly laid stone covered by thread bare pink wall-to-wall. The furniture wobbled apart with the slightest movement, and the rafters were suspended over very questionable, bowed two by threes. Except for the spectacularly unsanitary bathroom and the miniscule sleeping rooms, the kitchen, storage and eating area occupied one forty-foot-square room arranged around a yak-dung pot belly stove. The entire house felt as if it would pitch over the embankment if someone sneezed. While I was eating a lunch of spaghetti and red sauce; every bite of which tasted as if dribbled with gasoline, a member of an Indian team with altitude sickness heaved his guts out for a full five minutes ... into the sink. A skanky pony with an alarming skin infection slunk around the front door and was fed with a bucket that was returned to its' rightful place, our kitchen.

It was April 28, 2010, at 16,000 feet, and son Kurt and I were two days from completing a goal that we had set seven years previous. Our years' long plan was to have an adventure, anywhere in the world, in celebration of Kurt's high school graduation. After arriving home from the Everest summit in 2008, I pitched Nepal and a Base Camp trek.

"That's baller dawg!" he replied. Rough translation: "sounds good to me, oh wonderful dad-of-the-century."

Though well-travelled for a kid, Kurt had never been to the developing world. I wanted him to rub shoulders with the fascinating people and lands, made all the more dramatic by the backdrop of the Himalaya, the biggest mountains on earth. I will not deny that I also wanted to go back to the mountains, for the first time as a non-climber.

I had gotten out of shape in the months after achieving my years' long goal of summiting Everest. For the first time in many years I had no big goal, mountain or otherwise, on the horizon. In fact, I had decided to retire from high-altitude mountaineering. I relished the Base Camp hike with Kurt to have an adventurous, but safe, month together before he left for college and the rest his life. I also hoped it would put a burr under my saddle to get back in shape and more importantly, find some direction for my suddenly rudderless future. I needed a "next."

We had had an adventure just getting out of Dodge. An Icelandic volcano had decided to blow its' lid the day of our departure from Boston, cancelling all flights to and from Europe. We were scheduled to fly Boston to London to Bahrain to Kathmandu. Luckily, high-blood-pressured phone calls, frantic driving, and a few arguments later, we were re-routed to New York City and Doha, Quatar, and actually arrived in Nepal several hours earlier than we would have via our original itinerary.

It was fascinating for me to see the developing world, this time through Kurt's eyes. After arriving in Kathmandu, and surviving the demonic sacred-cow dodging cab drive to Hotel Tibet, we walked to Thamel. This touristy area of shops and restaurants was ringed by the palace formerly occupied by the two hundred and forty year monarchy on one side, and on the other sides by slum. Near the palace we passed eighty foot pines, the daytime home to humongous two to three foot, upside-down hanging bats. A ten minute walk later, we arrived at the sidewalk where the professional pan-handlers plied their trade. This year the new hook for tourist dollars was to leave an eight-month-old infant on the sidewalk alone, in ninety degree heat, so passers-by would drop ten-rupee bills into a can. Kurt was horrified at this spectacle and throughout our three-week-trip would ask me if I thought the baby was still alive.

Fifty feet along was the street corner where the "huffers" lived — seven to twelve year-old boys, addicted to sniffing glue. Their life expectancy was no more than twelve because they habitually fell into the street and were run over by cabs. These urchins were deeply stained with dirt and filth and clothed in nothing but frayed loin cloths. They lived out their ephemeral existence in stark contrast to the meticulous cleanliness and natty get-up of the typical Kathmandu inhabitant. Kurt took it all in with stunned silence.

I lay awake listening to the calming city-sounds of the Kathmandu night while Kurt sawed logs, contemplating our reasons for being there. In addition to adventuring together, Kurt's goal included finishing his senior project (raising funds for a Nepali school started by my Everest teammate, Val Hovland in conjunction with the organization Room-To-Read (www.roomtoread.com). Kurt had researched and presented lectures and slide-shows to meet his fund-raising goal of $1000. Besides the planned fandango, my other mission involved delivery of a white cowboy hat requested by climbing partner Phinjo Sherpa. (Apparently, white cowboy hats are worn at weddings and other important events by the happnin' Sherpa male).

In the dark, I thought about how we have multiple missions or reasons for being in the well-lived life. I remembered back to my years of climbing — mountains for me were made of snow, ice, and rock — but to others they could include anything: a big goal, a personal trait that no longer serves, one of life's myriad difficulties, something within that needs setting free. Superstar climber Steve House in his book, *Beyond The Mountain*, simply states — "each of us has his own unique battle... my ice axe may be your paint brush." Now that I was done with high-altitude climbing expeditions, I wondered what my next "Everest" was. What was next? Chapter One, if you remember, is entitled "Dream Management" but the chapter could aptly but clumsily be named, "My Mission For One Speck Of Time." I hoped to gain some clarity on my future specks of time during the trek with Kurt, and, as I said, see Nepal through his eyes.

Kurt trained hard in advance of his trip. He knew from attending my presentations that the Base Camp trek ain't for sissies. He pounded the step mill into submission at Core Gym in East Greenwich, RI. He dropped twenty pounds and went from twenty minutes to ninety minutes on the sport-specific, torturous, never-ending uphill machine. He kept his grades up, maintaining National Honor Society status, and got a tutor for calculus. He had a mission but realized a mission is worthless without the hard work. A warrior loves his craft ... where have I heard that before?

"When you are facing in the right direction (read: mission), keep putting one foot in front of the other" (read: work)
— **Phinjo Sherpa**

In Namche Bazaar, Kurt, our porter Suchille, and I were taking a tour of the Sherpa Museum. In a replica Sherpa house I smashed my head on a low beam nearly causing me to lose consciousness. I was dizzy and off for several hours. Kurt laughed. I yelled at Kurt. Several days later in Deboche on an acclimatization day, I ordered a pizza with mushrooms which were evidently spoiled as it turns out. I was sick as a dog for four days and experienced the rotten egg breath made famous by tent mate Chip in 2008. Years ago I would have allowed those experiences to ruin at least a few days of our trek, but I had learned that both good things and bad make the journey of life memorable and rich. "It's the journey not the summit," some great philosophical genius once said (in chapter three of this book I believe). My point here is that ya gotta love the ups and downs. When everything is perfect there is minimal learning, and as Grandmother Foster often told me, "learning is life-long." Therefore the struggle is life-long. My mate Rob Scott was fond of saying "It's only an adventure if the outcome is unknown." The many "walk-abouts" I was lucky enough to have made over the years were memorable for the people, weather, fatigue, conditions and the adventure, not merely the summit.

Kurt had quickly gotten used to not having a smart-phone surgically attached to his finger tips and was enjoying the daily ritual of hiking, resting and sight-seeing. He breathed a sigh of relief when he was able to snap photos of uniformed Nepali school schoolchildren inside a classroom, a coup-de-grace for his senior presentation. Kurt and I had ups and downs on the trek, (we got along swimmingly ninety-five percent of the time) but it added texture to the trip. John Hunt, leader for the 1953 Everest expedition that put Hillary and Tenzing on the summit, said "If you cannot go back home from an expedition saying that the human experience was enriching, none of it makes any sense."

We hired Suchille Sherpa to porter our shared duffel from Lukla to Base Camp and back. He was twenty-one years old, single, with a girlfriend in Kathmandu, and came from a village about a two hour hike from Lukla. His family farmed potatoes, spinach, barley, and cabbage. At each meal and rest break he bowled us over with helpfulness. He couldn't do enough for us — including smothering us with condiments at tea-time (We didn't actually request ketchup with our coffee but we always had it ready, just in case.). He was barely five feet tall with stubby, but powerful legs. He wore blue jeans every day on our fifteen day trek. In his tiny rucksack he had toothbrush, one t-shirt, one long sleeve shirt, and one skimpy down jacket. His footwear choice was a pair of garish yellow and lime green Pumas sans socks and at least three sizes too big. Oddly enough, one night three days into the trek someone swiped them. The same teahouse from which Suchille's peds were swiped, had a classic "ugly American" who loudly proclaimed in front of an international crowd, "That's why we rule the world, because you can get a burger or a greasy breakfast anytime you freakin' want." I silently blamed the ugly American as this sneaker stealer. Anyway, Suchille used that minimal clothes rotation the entire trek whether it was twenty-five or eighty-five degrees, and he somehow remained cleaner and better smelling than did Kurt and I ... we who had two large backpacks and a super-sized duffel stuffed with REI togs and a CVS supply of health and beauty aids.

The Sherpas who make all expeditions possible — from carrying to cooking, to just being great teammates, are living models of hopeful enjoyment of the daily journey. Unlike support workers in Africa or South America who sometimes lie and squeeze money from climbers as much as they can get away with, Sherpas are genuinely happy and enjoy helping people. They have a way of paying it forward which stems from their belief in reincarnation, a belief that tells them that each well-lived and generous life-time brings them closer to nirvana. Watching how Suchille accepted each day's simple pleasures reinforced my belief that hope is in the helping.

"May travelers upon the road find happiness no matter where they go, and may they gain, without hardship, the goals on which their hearts are set. As long as space exists, as long as beings endure, may I too, abide, to dispel the miseries of the world"
— Shantideva 7th Century Indian Scholar

Kurt was so happy and thankful to arrive at 17,300 foot Everest Base Camp. He made his goal — one he had worked hard for. Upon arriving, he called his mom on the sat phone and excitedly proclaimed, "Mom, I actually got my first altitude headache." On the trek he kept me in stitches with his dead-on impersonations of Darth Vader and Saruman from Lord of The Rings. We jabbered non-stop about everything from the hair on his back, to his academic angst, to his stone-faced persona that elicited suspicion with airport security guards on three continents. Kurt even deciphered the origin of the Buddhist mantra, "Om Mani Padme Hum" (Hail the Jewel in the Lotus Flower).

He explained that the rare and beautiful lotus flower (Read: person on the 'climb' of life) only grows in the foulest swamps (Read: adversity).

We stayed at Base camp for one night in a tent adjacent to none other than Big Al Hancock who was making his second, and ultimately successful, attempt on the world's highest real estate. I presented Phinjo with his cowboy hat, which surprisingly, after being thrown about on planes and 'binered to the back of my rucksack for two dusty weeks, didn't have a scratch on it. Phi was thrilled.

Big Al accompanied us to Gorak Shep where we shared some momos and Fanta before Kurt and I left the glacial landscape and headed for Pheriche. Al went back to Base and continued his expedition. Our intent was to hammer the pace for three days and get the last ten a.m. flight from Lukla to Kathmandu. To accomplish this Kurt and I agreed to the rules — two days of exhausting hiking to Namche where we would need to hit the trail by four a.m. at the latest, to get to Lukla before the last flight. Kurt was pooped upon arrival at Nuru's Himalayan Hotel the first hard day. He was knackered when we finally crawled into Namche the second day. On the penultimate "summit" day, we levered ourselves out of bed at three a.m. and into the night air in Namche at three forty-five a.m. to await Suchille. I knew it would be touch and go for us to hightail it to Lukla in time, but it didn't help that Suchille was late rousting his carcass out of his sleeping bag. Kurt started out tired, started to drop behind at daybreak, and was suffering in a big hairy way by seven a.m. The only problem was we had three hours of hard trekking to go. Kurt had a choice: stop, drop, and whine (SDW), or, keep putting one foot in front of the other (BGS — bow to the god of suffering). I am proud to say he chose "BGS" with only occasional "W." I couldn't help him, no one could. I could only firmly but lovingly remind him to take care of himself — basics such as reapplication of sunscreen and staying hydrated. He had to come to an agreement with those pained seconds, minutes, and hours. The old saw in Buddhism is "wherever you go, there you are." It turned out that we missed the plane by an hour, but we didn't mind. In fact, I saw it as Kurt's finest hour.

> *"When the going gets tough ... get back on the yak."*
> — Dr. Tim Warren

We had time to kill in Lukla so Kurt and I found a good restaurant, wandered into shops, and people watched.

We flew to Kathmandu where those pesky fun-loving Maoists forced another city-wide strike forcing us, in turn, to subsist for three days on room service rice, Bollywood movies, and the twenty-four-hour cricket channel. We flew Kathmandu to Doha, Quatar then Doha to New York City then NYC to Boston. We were home.

Early in my chiropractic practice I was warned of the dangers of "post goal mortem." In other words, establishing and striving for a business or personal goal and once attaining it, feeling empty and un-fulfilled. To avoid this condition, it was advised to set another goal that got the blood boiling. The procedure was not to wait until the previous goal was attained, but rather, just before. I hadn't done this after summiting Everest and was foundering as a result. Did I find a new mission that set my blood to boil? Did I find my next "Everest" at Base Camp, in Kurt's Vader imitations, in bad mushroom pizza or in Suchille's choice of footwear? You betcha, my next "Everest" was set, it was writing this book.

"We walk in our moccasins upon the earth and beneath the sky as we travel on life's path of beauty. We will live a good life and reach an old age."
— Navajo Blessing

ACKNOWLEDGEMENTS

There are many people I would like to thank for all their support, love and encouragement throughout the journey of my life. In respect to crafting this book, I received invaluable assistance from many people but especially Rose Yehle, Lisa Tener, Jack Galvin, Betty Cotter, Linda Remick, Dr. Jay (PKX) Manning, Anne Babineau, Alan Greco of Alan Greco Design, Sharon Hanson, Joanne Dempsey, Pat Piscopio, Big Wicked Al Hancock, Craig John, Dr. LuAnne Freer, Tom Sjogren, Eric Simonson, Mike Hamill, and Ang Jangbu Sherpa. The front cover photograph was taken by Nicole Messner (and is Dave Hahn), the back cover photos were taken by Bob Lowry and Bob Fontaine of Bob Fontaine Photography. Inside photos were shared from Val Hovland, Nat Smelser and Justin Merle.

In the mountains I benefitted greatly from living and learning with my rental units, Allan and Debora Warren; my sibs, Dan Warren and Liz Tuchler; Dana Millar, Rob (Dickweed) Scott, the SOB mountaineering club, Bob DeGregorio, Scott Schnackenberg, and Craig John; Kurt Warren, Palmer Dogface Warren, Bob Kancir, Sue Lansil, Chris Heberg and Lieth MacArthur, among many others.

I wish to thank my Everest homies for making the memories lifelong; Ang Jangbu Sherpa, Phinjo Sherpa, Mingma Sherpa, Jamling Bhote, Donchere, Tunang, Mark Tucker, Ciprian Popovisciu, Vance Cook, Ryan Campbell, Rohan Freeman, Serge Massad, Crazy Joe Yanuzzi, Val Hovland, Jaroslaw Hawrylewicz, Dean Smith, Lobsang Sherpa, Justin Merle, Adam Janakowski, Scott Parazynski, Ari Paress, Bob Pospishil, Casey Grom, Kurt Wedburg, Mike Andrews, Jim and Kate Swetnam, Dr.'s Gary and Willi, Monty Smith, Wildman Bob Lowry, Phunuru Sherpa, Panuru Sherpa, Danuru Sherpa, Dawa Sherpa, Kami Sherpa, Jim Harter, Greg and Nicole (Reinhold) Messner, George Shaw, Kuo Yu Cheng, Dave Hahn, Eric Simonson, Passang Rinjing Sherpa, Karma Rita Sherpa, Dr. LuAnne Freer and the staff of Base Camp ER, the staff of IMG ABC, the staff of IMG Camp Four, the staff on the BC trek, Alan Arnette, Walter Laserer, and Eben Reckord.

Also big thanks to the 2007 Everest home-boys and home girls: Phu Tashi Sherpa, Jean Ricard, TA Loeffler, Nat Smelser, Dave Schlimme, the bald guy who doesn't want to be identified, Robert Goh, Mike Haugen, Big Al, Russ Lamb, Sam Kay, Ray Kopcinski, John Deans,

Dagny Veitch, Chris Bergum, Ang Yau Choon, Mike Nixon, Nima Karma Sherpa, Fernando Palacios,Samduk Sherpa, Benjamin Salazar Cortes, Gentleman Jim Waldron, Andre Bredenkamp, and Ang Namgya.

"So ... be your name Buxbaum or Bixby or Bray
Or Mordecai Ali Van Allen O'Shea,
You're off to Great Places!
Today is your day!
Your mountain is waiting.
So ... get on your way!"
— Dr. Seuss

Contact Dr. Tim Warren at www.lessonsfromeverest.com
Or at 2797 Post Rd. Warwick RI 02886 USA
Phone: 401-738-6477 Fax: 401-738-7310
Presentations, Seminars, Keynotes and Slide Shows
Bulk Book Sales available.